CANADIAN
VOICES

Volume One

AN ANTHOLOGY OF PROSE AND POETRY

BY EMERGING CANADIAN WRITERS

Published by:

BookLand Press
6021 Yonge Street, Suite 1010
Toronto, Ontario M2M 3W2
Canada
www.booklandpress.com

Project coordinator: Trade Architects (Canada) Inc.

Printed and bound in Canada.

Library and Archives Canada Cataloguing in Publication

Canadian voices : an anthology of prose and poetry
by emerging Canadian writers.

ISBN 978-0-9784395-5-2

1. Canadian literature (English) — 21st century.

PS8251.1.C36 2009   C810.8'006   C2009-905893-6

TABLE OF CONTENTS

PART ONE: PROSE

PART TWO: POETRY

PART ONE
PROSE

SNORKELLING IN THE INDIAN OCEAN
by Dahn Batchelor

IT WAS A WARM, humid day in the first week of May 2005 when my wife, Ayako, and I decided that we would go snorkelling in the Indian Ocean, off the Indonesian island of Bali.

We are both accomplished swimmers and felt at ease as the crew of two took us in their four-and-a-half metre boat with its two powerful outboard motors, out into the ocean, six kilometres from land. We were told that that the boats we saw in the distance were at a favourite snorkelling spot where many fish could be seen.

When we reached that location, our boat stopped and Ayako and I jumped into the water. I weighed 124 kilograms at that time and as my wife tells it, after I hit the water, the swell almost swamped the boat. But then she also lied when she told her friends at home that when I stepped out of the Dead Sea in Israel, the level of that body of water dropped as much as two centimetres.

After an hour of us trying to catch fish in our hands—that was a time-wasted effort—we decided to get back into the boat. My Japanese-born wife is much lighter than I am and she had no difficulty climbing up the ladder and getting into the boat. I, on the other hand, being much heavier than my wife and disabled to

boot—well let's just say that her efforts were not unlike her climbing onto our bed whereas my efforts were as if I was trying to climb the CN Tower on my hands.

The ladder only went to the gunwale and not above it. It was like trying to climb onto a roof when the ladder only goes to the eavestrough. To make matters worse, because I am disabled, I didn't have the strength in my legs to push myself up the ladder. Since it didn't extend beyond the gunwale, I couldn't pull myself up the ladder either.

The two men, each weighing at least 90 kilograms, grabbed my wrists and tried to pull me up. The combined weight of the men and me was at least 304 kilograms. It was obvious to us all that the boat was about to capsize. The men let me go and ran to the centre of the boat and I dropped back into the water.

Meanwhile, the snorkellers on the other boats nearby began videotaping what they were seeing. They knew it was for real but unless they videotaped what was unfolding before them, no one at home would ever believe that particular tale from the South Seas.

One of our crew jumped into the water beside me with a life jacket in hand and told me to put it on. This I did. Then he told me to lie on my back. This I did also and suddenly, he placed a rope in my hand and said, "We are going to tow you back to land."

I thought I could hear birds in the distance. It wasn't birds I was hearing. It was the people on the other boats laughing. This was becoming extremely humiliating.

Within a minute, I could hear the two outboard motors starting up, and suddenly I felt a sharp tug of the rope against my closed fists as the boat, which was approximately eighteen metres from me, began to haul me back to land.

As we crashed through the waves, it became apparent to me that my bathing suit—boxer shorts actually—was slowly bunching around my knees. If my shorts came off, I would never find them, as they were almost identical to the colour of the ocean. The prospect of being dragged nude onto a crowded public beach wasn't something I was too keen to experience. If I could hear 'birds' laughing in the Indian Ocean, the flock of them at the beach would be deafening.

I reached down to my shorts with one hand in an attempt to pull them back up but to no avail. Then I decided that if I raised my knees up to my chest, my shorts would not come off and be left behind while I was being dragged through the water heading northward. The drag my body was creating as it was pulled through

the water was bad enough, but my wife said later that when I put my knees up, it was like watching a storm surge approach the island.

I've told my wife a million times, "Don't exaggerate!"

Finally, the drag was too much and the rope was pulled out of my hands and there I was, floating on my back while the boat continued towards Bali. My wife called out to the crew that they had left her husband behind.

They came back for me and stopped; then one of the men told me to swim to the ladder. When I reached it, he told me to hang onto the ladder as tightly as I could because they were going to take me back to land with me hanging onto the ladder. By now, I was too exhausted to climb up the ladder, so I hung onto a rung just at the surface of the water.

The boat travelled sixteen kilometres an hour at this stage of my adventure, but half the time I was submerged under the bow wave that meshed with the ocean waves. Worse yet, my feet were only centimetres from the propeller on the port side of the boat and I knew that if I let go of the ladder, my feet would hit the propeller while the prop was spinning about with its meat-grinding revolutions.

About half an hour later, the boat suddenly stopped. The two men jumped into the water and much to my surprise, they were in shallow water. It only went up to their waists. They began to push me up the ladder while my wife pulled on my wrists. As I flopped into the boat, I could hear the people on nearby boats, chirping away in fits of laughter as their video cameras continued to record what to them had to be the funniest images they had ever seen.

When we finally reached the beach, I jumped out of the boat and lay flat on my back. I was totally exhausted and needed a rest. Within minutes, two people from one of the other boats approached me and while looking down at my exhausted body, one of them said with a sympathetic smile, "Hi. We're from Greenpeace. We're going to help you back into the water."

An adaptation of "The Donkey Story"
LUCKYONE
by Kathleen Betts

"WE SHOULD DIG THE well before we get too thirsty." That was the motto old farmer Dino would spout to inspire his son Pepito with his prized donkey, Luckyone, along with his other dedicated workers, to get on with it lickety-split when flavour-of-the-month notions flooded his head. Outfitted with an untamed imagination and a cream-of-the-crop view of himself, Dino had an uncanny ability to charm the people around him into getting his work done, like dinner. To say the least, his leadership style was noteworthy.

Farmer Dino loved his farm and above all, he adored flaunting the fruits of the toil of labourers who marched to the beat of his drum. Dino's mind tripped into high gear one day, over a conversation he had with a crony. The perfect, precision long furrows Pepito and Luckyone had ploughed prompted him to conceive the idea to streamline his operations.

To keep his farm running as tickety boo as it did in his head, he decided to shake things up a bit and sneak some new blood into the midst of his workers. He decided to hire himself a high-falootin right-hand man. Sure, it would be a kick in the gut to Pepito who had grown up devoting his most cherished years to the farm, with

the faithful help of Luckyone, the donkey, and the rest of their family and friends.

Farmer Dino rallied his troops with an all too familiar, "We should dig the well before we get too thirsty." It became his vision to hand pick a high-falootin right-hand man to streamline operations, as any other modern farmer would.

"It is what it is," he exclaimed as he bamboozled Pepito and others in an attempt to usher in fresh blood. Bewildered, Pepito truly believed his father would soon flip-flop back to his quasi-senses and abandon this notional structure he was imposing, without considering the mass confusion, and the crushing blow to morale it would inflict on the loyal crew.

"It's going to be okay," Pepito spoke out aloud to reassure himself and the others. "Soon there will be a new flavour of the month and we'll be ready to dig that well instead."

Dino, steadfast and charismatic forged onward in oblivion to the devastating effects his plan would have and with utter disregard for the effect on the relationship he had with Pepito and the others who had toiled with pride and integrity for the good of the farm.

Dino introduced his new wonder, Charlie, who fit perfectly into the devilish image concocted in his brain. As Charlie was no stranger to dirty work, Dino knew he was just the right guy to step into it on the farm. In tandem, Dino and Charlie chimed a banal, "We should dig the well before we get too thirsty."

Shortly after Charlie's arrival, dependable old Luckyone awoke in horror one day, to find herself in a dark, dank, dreary place, way down the bottom of a well. Beleaguered, Luckyone cried out, to get the attention of anyone who could come to her rescue. Dino heard the commotion and went running with Charlie right on his heels, to see what it was all about. Reeking of irony and bilge, Luckyone looked up at them from the depth of a derelict well she had dutifully helped to dig for a gung ho flavour of the month that Farmer Dino had sampled years earlier.

Farmer Dino and Charlie had to think quickly of a way to get out of this pickle. With a total disregard for life, Dino decided to just fill the neglected well with dirt. It was just too much trouble to find a way to lift Luckyone out. She was old anyway and wasn't going to fit in well with the new streamlined operation Dino had envisaged.

Farmer Dino sent Pepito out on a wild goose chase while

Charlie rounded up the troops to help them to fill the pit, with Luckyone still at the bottom. Unknown to the neighbours who had rallied to help with the shovelling, Charlie had furtively led Luckyone to the depression in the land and tipped her over the edge.

Isn't the devil always hidden in the details? While some of those lesser-informed shovellers wondered fleetingly if there might be something else that could be done, they regarded the farmer as a leader among them and most, simply resigned to go with the flow. They did not actually shovel, but they stood by and watched the others abet in the atrocity. After all, it was Farmer Dino's idea. If Dino wanted the well filled, what else could they do? To get the whole nasty deed over and done with as quickly as possible, some of them actually grabbed their shovels and began to fling filth and muck into the hole.

Luckyone was horrified and screeched in terror as she realized what was happening. The mob of shovellers had to be strong in their resolve to continue what they had started. With their conscience dangling by a thread, some felt remorseful about the obvious fate of the faithful old donkey.

Much to their relief, Luckyone finally calmed down as though in acquiescence to the morose destiny in store. Presumably, she was too exhausted to fight any longer. Not having to see her or hear her pleas to their mercy made it easier for the mob to continue without having to face those niggling pinches of guilt.

As the dirt continued to pour, Farmer Dino mustered the gall to peer down into the hole again to see what progress his team had made towards the plan. He was astounded. With each shovel load that the band of followers dumped onto her back, the sanguine burro was doing something Farmer Dino had never imagined possible. There stood Luckyone, strong and calm, shaking off the dirt as it landed on her head and back. Seemingly, Luckyone sensed from afar, the support and quiet encouragement from her friends on the farm as well as the unbearable longing that Pepito would suffer if she were to succumb to the wicked plan and took strength from it. While the throng of adherents continued to shovel, Luckyone kept shaking it off and taking a step up. Soon, she stepped right up over the edge and trotted off to find Pepito.

The shovellers gathered around the old well, gave themselves a congratulatory round of pats on the back for the achievement of having "helped out." Dino and Charlie even gave each other a big

ol' high five for masterminding the rescue. Some struggled though, with the evil sense of conspiracy and betrayal in which they had been willing to partake.

What finally happened with faithful old Luckyone was that she came back and vengefully gnawed off her rightful pound of flesh from Dino for trying to bury her alive. The gash got infected and Farmer Dino became so sick from the toxicity that he had to retire from the farm that he had professed to love so much.

When you try to cover your luckyone, it comes back to bite you.

An excerpt from
the travel memoir "Into Africa: The Return"
THE CANOPY WALK
by Yvonne Blackwood

WITH EVERY STEP I took, the narrow rope bridge rocked and swayed like an empty hammock on the beach being pummelled by the west wind. It creaked like an old wooden ship on the verge of falling apart. Then it hit me. I was suspended 30 metres in midair, high above the thick, lush rain forest in Ghana, supported merely by a network of ropes and cables, and a narrow 30-centimetre board with slender metal bars on either side used as a footpath. I wobbled in the middle of the first of seven stages of the bridge with no one to hold on to and no one to share my anxieties. The bridge was 350 metres long.

I had no concept of distance at this point. Then from the recesses of my mind, I recalled a fragment of sports trivia that a football field is about 109 metres long. It meant that the bridge where I stood was longer than three football fields put together! My salivary glands dried up instantly. My throat began to constrict. I became paralyzed.

After a few moments, I summoned up enough courage to continue the tortuous walk, staggering along the walkway as if intoxicated. My heart began to pound like a Kpanlogo drum and my

body heated up far beyond the normal 37 degrees Celsius. My sweat glands exploded and perspiration streamed down my face and back. I held a large handkerchief in my right hand. It was a good time to blot the moisture, but I had pressed it unalterably against the rope and dared not let go to wipe my face. The sweat continued to flow. It dripped into my eyes and onto my lips.

Gripping the ropes on either side of the narrow bridge, I kept going, knowing that my life depended on its support. I continued to put one heavy unsure foot in front of the other, slowly, and with calculation.

But before long, I felt another panic attack surging to the surface and the dryness in my throat intensified tenfold. I had six-and-a-half more stages of the bridge to complete. It seemed the walk would take me forever. I now had a strong sense that primates and other wild creatures were waiting longingly beneath the deceptive canopy of shrubbery for lunch — my head, my limbs and my organs!

Dear God, what have I done?

My legs became weaker and weaker. I was breathing in spurts, my heart racing faster than a cheetah rushing at its prey. How did I get myself into this mess? I CANNOT do this. I can't go any farther; I must go back.

The words of Robert, our guide, roared inside my head. "If you're afraid of heights, don't look down; just look straight ahead." Suddenly, the bridge creaked louder than I'd heard it before and it swayed wider than it had ever done.

Oh God, I'm done for now!

I clung tighter to both sides of the thick rope bridge until my knuckles hurt. I wanted to cry, to pee, to do anything that would relieve the tension, anything to eradicate the nightmare, anything except to be on the bridge. I didn't look down; I couldn't even if I'd wanted to.

I decided that I wouldn't suffer anymore; I would swivel around and retrace my steps, not an easy movement on a narrow bridge that swayed constantly. It would be like turning on a dime, so to speak.

I twisted my head slightly to glance at where I'd started this crazy, daring feat. To my horror, my cousin Marie, a heavy-set, 42-year-old woman, was already on the bridge, walking precariously toward me! That explained the wider sways and louder creaks.

Damn, I'm screwed.

I had Hobson's choice now; I could either leave or continue. Choice number one was not an option; there was no getting off, unless I wanted to fulfill the zestful desires of the ferocious animals waiting, lurking beneath the bushes.

Going back was out of the question too. Something else Robert had said flooded into my head. "Only one person is allowed on the bridge at a time." The person ahead of me would've completed stage one and moved onto the second leg by now. In another few moments, Marie would arrive at my spot and another person would step onto the bridge. With only four members of the group ahead of me, and Marie behind me, six tourists and two guides were still waiting to get on. I couldn't ruin this once-in-a lifetime adventure for the rest of the group. I had to move forward.

As I thought more about the situation, my fear changed to anger.

Wait until I see Charles Ansah again; if I ever do, I'll strangle him with my bare hands! He got me into this...

Robert was medium build, about twenty-four, and dressed in a crisp khaki suit. He stood facing the group, surrounded by tall trees that partially blocked out the sunlight, as he gave us a well-rehearsed overview of the rain forest.

"This part of the forest consists of 360 square kilometres and is conserved with the agreement and help of the Ghanaian government and some world organizations. There are over 40 species of large mammals such as elephants and Royal antelopes in this forest. There are over 300 different species of birds, 400 species of butterflies and hundreds of insects. There are also reptiles."

Peabody shivered and looked around with wide bulging eyes. She hates reptiles.

"Don't worry P, I'm sure you won't come close to any," I whispered and squeezed her hand.

"There are more than 200 species of plants per square hectare," Robert said. "Some of the trees in the forest are over 60 metres high. Most of the animals in this forest are nocturnal so I can't guarantee that you'll see any today. But don't worry; they already know you're here; some can pick up your scent two kilometres away. Any questions?"

An uneasy feeling crept over me. Hungry wild beasts were watching us but we couldn't see them! Robert gave us more information and told us about the canopy walkway. I listened attentively at first, then tuned out. He surveyed the group. There

were six Caucasians (four Swedish girls in their teens and a middle-aged Dutch couple), three virile, black American men, cousins Peabody and Marie, and me. Robert was the main guide and Sam, 18 years old, was his assistant. No one posed a question, so Robert continued.

"Please do not disturb the animals by making too much noise. Do not disturb the plants by stepping on the roots or by shaking the branches. Many of the plants in this forest have valuable medicinal value. Some are used to make soaps, perfumes, and of course, drugs."

We moved on, walking single file behind Robert, into the heart of the forest. Along the way, Robert pointed out several trees and gave details about them. At one spot we came upon a huge tree trunk in our path.

"This trunk has been lying here for more than 10 years," Robert said.

"How did this huge log get here?" one of the Swedish girls asked.

"Logging was big business in this forest at one time and a logging company chopped down this tree. But when they realized that it was impossible to transport such a large tree out of the forest, they left it here."

We continued until we reached the entrance to the world-renowned Canopy Walkway. Robert stopped to explain the rules before we were allowed on.

"The Canopy Walkway bridge is 350 metres long and is suspended 30 metres above the forest. It is divided into seven sections and has six platforms. Only one person is allowed on each section at a time. Once you reach the mid-point of a bridge section, another person can start walking. You can only go one way. The bridge will sway while you're on and it will creak, but don't worry, it is safe."

"Anyone ever fall off?" the Dutch man asked and laughed nervously, exposing cigarette-stained teeth.

"Not that I know of."

I hardly think he would divulge that information, you blockhead.

"The oldest woman to do this walk was 87 years old and the oldest man was 96," said Robert. "He was an ex-serviceman from England. Who will go on first?" He scrutinized the group, a challenging look on his face.

Two of the black American men decided to exhibit their

"machomanship" and volunteered to begin the walk. Cousin Peabody piped up that she would be third. The other American said he would be fourth. I quickly volunteered to take spot number five. I didn't want to be first but most certainly didn't want to be last either. Marie opted for spot number six and so the adventure began.

I thought about Marie heading my way, and of the other eight people waiting anxiously to begin the daring walk. What kind of message would I send them if I backed out? What kind of respect would I receive if I showed cowardice now? I would ruin everything for them. No, despite my fear and trepidation, I had to go through with it.

I took several deep breaths, whispered a prayer, mustered up every ounce of courage in my being, and kept on going, hanging onto the ropes as the bridge continued its spineless dance. The boards creaked and groaned, and in the quietness of the rainforest with only the chirping of birds, the creaking was magnified many times. I focused on the words of the guide, "Don't worry; it is safe."

Exotic butterflies flitted by, butterflies one could only imagine based on illustrations in fairytale books. The rope bridge in the Indiana Jones movie, *Raiders of the Lost Ark,* paled in comparison to this one. Finally, I consoled myself that others had done the walk before me and had survived. Didn't Robert say a 96-year-old man had done it? Why would the good Lord choose my turn to snap the bridge?

Bearing that in mind, I plodded on, looking straight ahead until I came upon the first platform. At the end of each section of the bridge, platforms were firmly anchored to giant trees 100 to 400 years old. I stepped off the bridge, stood on the first platform, and exhaled.

It was only here that I had the confidence to look down and over the forest for the first time. A panorama of magnificent emerald foliage unfolded before my eyes. The view was spectacular. Such a view as could not be seen from the ground. The flora was a canopy of trees of varying sizes, ages and colour spectrum, all competing fiercely for the sunlight and the rain. Everything seemed so organized, so meticulously planned. It was Mother Nature at her best and I marvelled at the power of the creator.

Soon, I stepped onto the second bridge and continued the walk, gaining more confidence as it swayed and creaked, but never looking down until I placed my feet onto the other platforms. There, I took it all in like a drug, then moved on.

I was one-third the distance of the final stretch of the seventh bridge when I looked straight ahead and saw Peabody and the three black Americans standing under a small covered platform. They had completed the walk and had positioned themselves to cheer the rest of the group along. I grinned from ear to ear and knew there would be no turning back for me; the mission would be accomplished.

Out of the tranquility, and without any warning, a booming clap of thunder rocked the forest. It scared me so; I jumped and almost fell off the bridge. Raindrops, the size of ping-pong balls fell intermittently and splattered on my head and arms.

No, it can't be. It can't rain now. I'm still on the bridge!

JOEY AND THE TURTLE
by Alison E. Bruce

THE TURTLE TOLD ME my sister was dying.

Three years younger and at least two inches shorter than I, Joey was, nevertheless, my big sister. Somewhere between being the baby who ousted me from my place as centre of the universe to the adult that made it her mission to keep me employed, she outstripped me in political savvy, business acumen, and general bossiness.

Of course, it didn't help that I was the "space cadet" of the family. Plagued by chronic ear infections that culminated in becoming half deaf at age nine, it was easier to slip into a world of my own making—less frustrating to smile and nod than ask, for the umpteenth time, "What was that?"

I first noticed that I was losing the advantage of primogeniture in high school. In Grade 10, Joanne joined the drama club and stage-managed every production from then until she graduated. Everyone knew her. Most people knew me as Joanne's sister—or so it seemed to me at the time. I loved her, admired her, but I admit to a touch of resentment at being the "second sister." That's why I started calling her "Joey"—to annoy her. Like the Brits calling the Americans Yanks, she adopted the nickname with pride, and I, a softie at heart,

let her think that the name was a gift, not an epithet.

When Joey started her own business, I named that, too. I helped her create marketing materials. I stood in line with her at the registration office. Until she actually signed the forms, I had no idea whether or not I was going to be a partner.

Later, Joey told me that if I had asked...

I replied, if she had asked...

Neither of us said a word at the time, so Joanne became the sole owner of BelleFare Communication Services. Not that it would have changed much. She still would have been the boss.

Thanks to Joey, I learned print layout and design. Thanks to me, she had someone who could write whatever she needed, whenever she needed it. It worked. I worked. When I didn't work as much as I needed to, she found me contracts outside of BelleFare to keep the money flowing. Having a "big sister" became advantageous—even amusing, since we were getting to the age when looking older wasn't as much fun anymore.

I remember the day things started to unravel.

It was a cold but sunny January afternoon. BelleFare was doing well enough to have moved out of Joey's home and into its own office. Business was good enough for me to be salaried. Our parents had recently moved to town, so Dad dropping by wasn't uncommon. Usually he brought coffee. That day he brought the news that Mum was waiting in the van and wanted to talk to us.

That's the day we found out that Mum had inoperable, aggressive lung cancer. Less than a month later, Joey was diagnosed with breast cancer, and we found out that Dad had a tumour on one of his kidneys.

Spring 1999 was marked by surgeries and other medical procedures, capped by a family trip to Florida by way of the Georgia coast. Mum had a wig which came off in the van to reveal a halo of transparent silver fuzz. Dad had a functioning kidney again. Joey had the maps and a determination not to let her children know how scared she was.

September: Another sunny day at the office. Joey had recently returned to work after recovering from a course of radiation therapy. Dad came in to tell us Mum was waiting in the van and wanted to talk to us.

That's the day we found out that the chemotherapy wasn't effective. Mum was dying. What I remember most was a mushroom pushing its way up through the tarmac. We'd tried to get rid of

it several times, but it kept cropping up. Like Mum's cancer, it wouldn't go away.

Life took on a surreal quality. Within the space of a few days, I was told my mother was dying and I discovered I was pregnant. I was sad for my mother, happy to be having a second child, and worried about both impending events. I was angry at my mother, at the world in general, and at my partner, specifically, for what I saw as a lack of support in my time of need. He might have been the only one who openly felt that anger, because for everyone else I had to be strong.

I especially had to be strong for Joey. She had recently had her own mortality thrown up in her face. As if that wasn't bad enough, Mum died on Joey's birthday. It was too much like an omen.

Another thread unravelled shortly after my son was born. Mere hours after the doctor took the staples out from my c-section, my incision burst open. The same night, a section of our apartment ceiling collapsed. The next thing I knew, my common-law marriage fell apart and I was living with my sister. She took care of me for two weeks. Then she arranged for me to move in with Dad because she figured we needed each other. Besides, Joey and I had tried living together in university — bad idea.

Bad or not, less than a year later I was living with her again so that she could leave continuing care and be at home with her children.

Joey's cancer metastasized and started attacking her bones. After the first radiation treatments, she almost died because the painkillers masked a rupture in her colon.

That's when I met the turtle.

Part of my reputation as a space cadet rests on my interest in all things psychic and paranormal. I embarked on a Tarot self-study program when I was sixteen, and added astrology, comparative mythology, and animal guides as I went along. The turtle is a healer. I gave Joey a turtle figure as a talisman. When I sat in ICU watching the bi-pap machine pump air into her, I felt the turtle, and I knew she wasn't going to die . . . not yet.

Joey and the turtle fought cancer for three more years. There were some close calls in there, but there were also ceasefires.

After the first recovery, Dad, the kids, and I, moved closer to Joey and her girls so I could take care of her without living with her. The path between our two townhouses was like a corridor connecting two wings of the same house.

We took a family trip to Florida by way of Tybee Island, Georgia. One of my fondest memories is sitting on the deck overlooking the beach, watching the sun rise as we drank coffee. We had been there on our last trip with Mum, and Joey, in particular, felt in touch with Mum there.

We went to Europe together—I, Joey, three young kids, and the old man.

At home, Joey and I took turns reading aloud and completed the *Lord of the Rings* and the first few Harry Potter books. We continued to work. I set up a movable work station using a discarded microwave stand, so Joey's computer could move from bed to lift chair with her. From her bed in the living room, she designed conference and festival programs and a fire fighters' pin-up calendar. We adjusted life around her illness, but life went on.

There were also long stretches of hospital stays, for radiation and chemotherapy, surgery, and recovery from infections. I became familiar with the route from Guelph to Hamilton where Joey's oncologist and surgeon practised. I spent hours on the road, usually driving my sister's green Echo with the turtle talisman hanging from the mirror. I also got adept at text messaging. Text messages were a lot cheaper than long distance calls. Joey would send me reminders of what she wanted me to bring her. Then I'd pull over and text back that I was already halfway there—but did she want me to pick her up a coffee?

There came a point when I couldn't drive Joey to her appointments any more. Her bones were too brittle. We rode down in an ambulance. For once I didn't have to fight for the front seat, even though I wasn't driving. It was on one of those visits—the last one— that Joey was told that the treatments weren't working.

I refused to give up and Joey refused to give in. The fight continued, mostly for the sake of spending as much time as possible with her children. Then there came a point, once the last bit of BelleFare work was delivered and the first edit of my novel was completed, when it got too tiring.

Joey had a silver ankh that she used to wear on a chain. Medical procedures made wearing the chain impractical, so she wore it pinned to her gown instead. One day she undid the safety pin and gave the ankh to her eldest daughter, Sophie. Joey knew what I, for one, was unable to accept.

Hours later Joey had an episode. We'd been there, done that several times before, so, after calling 9-1-1, I calmly gathered medications, reading material, and the other odds and ends that would make my sister comfortable when she was settled in hospital. Even when she slipped into a coma, as the paramedics prepared her for transport, I didn't give up. Joey had been to the brink before and come back to us. The thought that she wouldn't make it hadn't entered my head.

For the next twenty-four hours, I was told at regular intervals that I should prepare myself for my sister's death. I wouldn't let them take her off assisted breathing. My own experience with asthma and fighting to take a breath made me horrified at the thought of Joey's being without air. On the other hand, if her heart stopped, I told them not to resuscitate. It was my one concession.

Joey wasn't the only one with a hospital bag. I spent so much time in waiting rooms, I had my own kit with a book to read, a notebook to write in, and a sketchpad and crayons in case I had the children with me.

I took out the sketch pad while I sat with Joey. I drew her a turtle and used a couple of pieces of medical tape to put it on the wall.

For a while, I stood by her bed, holding her hand.

"It's up to you now," I told her. "I'll take care of you forever if you want. Your company is payment enough. But, if you're tired and want to go, I'll understand."

After a while I sat down and drew the turtle diving for a treasure chest.

"Whatever you most want is in the chest," I told Joey, taping the second drawing up. "The turtle will get it for you."

That's when I knew. Since Joey was in a coma, the turtle told me.

A couple of hours later, I brought my nieces, Sophie and Claire, to visit their mother. I seem to remember our singing to her, but I can't be sure. We were all in a fog at the time. I remember noticing that Joey's heart monitor was fluctuating. Someone came in and turned off the alarm. Soon after that we were asked to step out. Later we were allowed back for a final goodbye.

I must have gathered up the turtle pictures because I still have them. I still have the turtle talisman from the car, and a collection of turtles given me by friends and family since.

Being the space cadet I am, I imagine Joey is with the turtle, on a beach with Mum and a fresh cup of coffee, watching the sun rise.

WORN-AWAY EDGES OF REALITY
by Altug Cakmakci

JIMMY GOT HIMSELF A new laptop on the day he got out of the asylum. The teenaged shop assistant had braces on his teeth and Jimmy couldn't understand him clearly when the guy mumbled on about the machine's technological features — but the laptop was a bargain for sure. Buying the thing was a reasonable action, Jimmy thought, just like Dr. Richardson repeatedly and deliberately had urged him to do.

"Always take reasonable actions," she'd say in an artificially calm tone when talking to Jimmy during one of their discovery sessions. Jimmy would typically stay silent. But once, he raised his head and said to her face, "Fuck you" — imitating her disgusting, pale voice. Dr. Richardson noted Jimmy's reaction as an instinctive and positive step in his recovery process. So, cursing was probably good and preferred in a way, when you were actually expected and not punished to pee in your pants.

As he was about to enter his apartment, Jimmy saw Professor Herbert, who lived on the top floor and was also an ex-asylum resident. Jimmy said, "Hi," and the man returned his greeting almost silently. The professor, carrying a couple of books under his

arm, moved a few steps back to stand at a distance from Jimmy. The man looked annoyed. You could easily tell that he had gotten out of the nut house not long ago. Jimmy was used to the man's suspicious nature and he always expected the Professor to do something weird at any moment.

"I've got a new laptop, Professor." Jimmy showed the box he was carrying to the man. The Professor looked at the box, which only had a brand logo on it, and nodded silently.

"I'm planning to write stuff, things… I don't know… Maybe stories… Yeah, I can write short stories," said Jimmy as the Professor started climbing the stairs. "Professor, would you mind reading my stories? I would like someone, I mean someone with a proper education, to take a professional look at the stuff I write."

Professor nodded. "Yes," he added, like it was necessary to convince Jimmy. "It is good to have you back."

Jimmy rushed into his apartment, brewed himself a cup of coffee, unpacked the package, and sat in front of his laptop. He opened a new file that looked like a plain white sheet of paper except that it had a frame with a ruler and several colourful buttons — though Jimmy had no idea what those buttons did. He started writing with an emotion that warmed his chest, and realized that filling the empty spaces with words made him happy for no big reason. It was like hearing a song, an amusing wedding song in which a Gypsy plays his trombone and everyone dances around.

To Jimmy's surprise, writing was both entertaining and satisfying. Words poured out like lava from a crater, and he stormed through his story like everything in it happened in just one moment. Writing was possibly the next best thing to getting stoned, Jimmy thought. Once he began to fill up the paper with words — and he had no idea where they were coming from — he did not want to stop. He wanted those moments to last longer, so long that his life would be one long session of writing and he could wallow in the utmost pleasure of all pleasures.

The next day he took his story to the Professor, who asked him to come back in half an hour and closed the door in his face. Jimmy drank a cup of coffee while looking outside his apartment window. He knocked on the Professor's door exactly thirty minutes later.

"Your story does not have any spirit," said Professor Herbert. At first, Jimmy got upset and then he got furious, but he calmed himself down. The Professor had read more books than you could

see in a library, he thought. I should listen to him.

"So?" asked Jimmy, begging for an answer.

"I cannot describe it, but your story does not have any spirit," repeated the Professor, walking to his kitchen.

Jimmy looked at the pile of papers. He spent a few minutes trying to interpret the meaning of spirit. Maybe the Professor had used the word in another sense. Professor Herbert came back carrying two cups with steam rising over their brims. Jimmy could smell the tea from where he stood.

"Look, Jimmy," said Professor Herbert. "Writing fiction is not easy. I never wanted to try it myself, because there's a catch to it." He took a sip from his tea. "You can't write about others. If you do, you won't succeed. You have to write about yourself, but then it won't be fiction."

"So, what should I do?" asked Jimmy.

"I don't know, Jimmy. Maybe you should try writing like you are writing in Borges's book of sand — a book which has no pages but every word is in it."

Jimmy returned to his apartment confused.

One thing was for sure — Jimmy did not want to write about himself and his bloody life. But, on the other hand, what the Professor had said sounded right to him. It would be much easier to write about himself. Jimmy caught sight of the inevitable, but tried to postpone its arrival. But, how could he resist himself, knowing his own weaknesses?

Jimmy started smoking again. On his first puff, he remembered the evil nurse at the asylum. Every Friday night, she and her minions would go hunting, looking into every hole in his small room, moving the furniture here and there, to find a pack of cigarettes or a flask of rum. Whenever the evil nurse discovered Jimmy's cache, she would look at him, lower her eyebrows and make a gesture, which Jimmy interpreted as: "I'd stick this package up your ass if we were alone." He took another puff.

Just before Jimmy left the asylum, Dr. Richardson asked him to practise physically, mentally, and socially being part of society again. Jimmy had no will for the first and no idea about the last, but mental practice sounded reasonable. And writing was the best way to practise, wasn't it? Oh, how he longed for those pink pills now. Just one would ease him, pull away the tricky thoughts, and give him a good night's sleep, which was hard to get in the asylum with his maniac neighbour banging his head on the wall all night until

the watchman rushed over to distract the neighbour from banging in his own sentimental way by using a thick stick.

Everything happens for a reason, Jimmy thought. He opened a new file on his laptop and typed in the right-hand corner the date he arrived at the asylum.

"Fuck," said Jimmy. "This isn't a fucking letter." He deleted the date and wrote the first sentence on the empty sheet instead:

"They took me in through the rear door of the asylum with my hands cuffed at the back."

Dr. Richardson would ask who "They" were if she had the chance to read that sentence. She was good at asking questions with millions of possible answers. Jimmy hated questions with millions of possible answers as much as he hated fried chicken. Both made him want to throw up.

Remembering the asylum, he lost his appetite. In the asylum all the meals had a unique taste and smell. Jimmy sometimes thought that they were all actually made from the same stuff some sort of shit—but the cook was very talented in giving the same food different shapes and colours. Jimmy dunked his bagel into the glass of milk. Sesame and those little black seeds floated on the white liquid. He decided to stop drinking that glass of milk.

Jimmy knew stories of the distant past—naive but blurry— and he knew stories of yesterday—stories that had the smell of asylum meals. It is inevitable, he thought, and for a reason.

He remembered the first guy he saw at the asylum. His name was Oscar. He always walked around with these transparent tubes in his nose and pulled a small suitcase on wheels. He was a nice guy, but you couldn't speak to him for more than two minutes. After that, he would either bite you or start screaming like you were cutting his fingers, or whatever.

Jimmy remembered another guy who refused to change his underwear and another one who started crying whenever he saw Dr. Richardson. Jimmy remembered the day he was put in the white room and how that one hour seemed like a week to him. Then he remembered the day he was put in the yellow room, and then in the white room again. He began to write and with a similar passion. Maybe the Gypsy was not playing now, but the words were gurgling up to the surface more than they had been before.

He fell asleep. He had a bad dream about the asylum—you never have good dreams about places like that. When he got up, his heart was pounding heavily. For the first time in his life, he was

happy to be awake. The dream stood clear in his memory. He got back to his laptop and wrote down all the details. He got himself a bagel and a cup of leftover cold coffee from the kitchen. He was ready to write for the whole day. He expected to finish his story before the day ended.

Unfortunately, after a few pages and numerous words, he fell asleep again. Right away he was back in the asylum, but this time it didn't feel like a dream to Jimmy. It was more like how he felt a couple of days ago — before he was released. He tried to wake up, but could not manage it. He tried to get away, return to his apartment, but it all seemed impossible. Either his sleep was endless or he was not sleeping at all. What was happening to him now? Was he stuck in his writing, in his own reality? Dr. Richardson always told him that, by facing his own fears, he would face himself — that he would come closer to reality, his own reality.

"Look at what you did now, bitch," he yelled. Facing his fears had not helped him, rather had put him back in the lunatic circus. "I must think clearly," said Jimmy. "Am I myself or what I just wrote?" His heart was pounding heavily. "If I can decide which is true, I can escape this dark hole." He looked confident to himself. He cleared his mind and focused on the one question that started to shine like a comet in a bright summer night in his consciousness:

"Am I more real than the things I write?"

PRIMAL SUSPICIONS
by Mauro Cappa

A SNOWY DAY, NOVEMBER 27, 1968, and here I am at the Huit Manor, sipping a fresh cup of tea and sampling an assortment of tea biscuits to my heart's content. Stacey, my fondest friend is to my right, and to my left, Mr. Green the storyteller of storytellers. The teakettle whistles in the background as Mrs. Thompson, Edgar and Rachel's maid prepares more tea for the guests.

In a sombre mood, Rachel enters the living room and greets all the guests. In a soft tone, she announces the sad news that her husband Edgar has been murdered. Phoebe and Edward weep while the others drop their heads at the news. Though I expected this to be announced, it still shocked me. Rumour has it that Rachel cannot sustain the mansion on her own. With Edgar's untimely death and much of their fortune stolen, she desperately needs it to be sold. It has twenty rooms on three levels and numerous bedrooms have accommodated many guests over the years.

The mansion, well known in the area, sits on a sprawling estate in the countryside, near the Alps. It has ornate gargoyles and intricately carved ten foot tall mahogany entrance doors that lead to a massive circular foyer. In advance of the public announcement,

several friends and acquaintances had been hastily invited to this open house. And so, here we find ourselves, gathered in the formal and lavishly decorated stateroom, graciously being served English tea and biscuits.

Rachel spoke in honour of Edgar and what a kind man he was. "He was a perfect match for me. And I miss him dearly."

I whisper to Stacey, "She seems quite composed considering barely a month has passed since Edgar's murder." Stacey nods politely.

Rachel goes on to say, "He was fire for my soul and now he is gone so suddenly and mysteriously." As she spoke, the phone rang, a jarring interruption, and Mrs. Thompson promptly answers the call.

The maid re-enters the room and calls Rachel to the phone. I sympathize with Rachel's predicament. She is one of the most respectable persons I have ever known. Her amiable personality is her strongest attraction. Her piercing, tired eyes evoke a strength of character although recent events have worn her down and dulled her spark.

Further to this sudden death, the theft hit the Huits hard. The theft of millions of dollars made headline news. According to the newspapers, Edgar's body found soon after the robbery indicated he had been stabbed to death. The media reported the progress in the case daily. There had been no arrests until last week, when a man by the name of Ivan Drovna had been arrested. It soon became obvious that he was not the culprit, though he was a criminal. He ended up confessing to a whole different crime which involved shoplifting two televisions and a radio.

Once Rachel got off the phone she calls me into the kitchen. She begins her communication with, "I have some rather displeasing news. The police just called me..." She glances quickly around and continues, "Whoever murdered my beloved Edgar is in this house at this very moment. Because of the impending storm, the driving conditions are treacherous and the police are unable to get here to resume their questioning. Can you help me out with this investigation Charles, given you are an ex-police officer?"

With astonishment and bewilderment I reply, "I will do whatever I can for you."

I proceed with Rachel into the living room as she announces to the crowd that the police believe the murderer is present among us.

"Since my place is only accessible via a narrow and steep unpaved road that winds itself around the hills, and due to the winter storm blowing from the nearby mountains, it makes it impossible for the police to get here. So Charles will assist the police with the investigations and I want you to co-operate with him."

A disturbed and disquieted feeling settles over the guests. For a few agonizing moments they all stare at each other suspiciously, half expecting, even if naïvely, that the killer would come forward and confess in front of everyone with embarrassment.

As I gaze out the window to witness the drifting snow, I know this is going to be a very long evening. Stacey reads my mind and whispers to me, "Charles, this will not be an easy task..." Stacey looks down at her feet. Then she stares into my eyes as she continues, "Somehow though, we'll get through this, right?"

Although I am neither a professional investigator nor a detective, Stacey promises to assist me in tracking down the murderer and in reporting him to the police. I didn't know what the outcome would be. It is perhaps the snow spiralling out of control outside that causes my mind to wander or is it just the thought of having no idea what I am getting myself into? Either way it is going to be an arduous task to organize evidence and suspects. Anything or anyone could throw me off my mission. Stacey appears apprehensive and I feel like comforting her.

"All we need to do, is study our suspects." I state trying to ease her worry. I immediately turn my attention to the crowd of people.

It is Salley I notice first. She is a young, gorgeous, blonde-haired woman with a soft innocent face. Her smile could make anyone's day. She rolls her electrifying green eyes as I stare at her. I quickly turn away from her and set my eyes on the teacup. I don't believe she is the murderer. Her angelic face, her soft-spoken voice, her poise and dignity -any mother would be proud of her!

Mr. Green blinks rapidly as he looks down at the floor. He seems a little nervous and I must admit, I am as well. He is concerned about something, but of what? Although I rule him out as a suspect, who knows? He could very well be the killer, since he does seem nervous. I decide to stick with my instincts at this point as they have served me well in the past.

Brock, an electrical engineer, his thick tough hands speak of manual work, fiddles with a black fountain pen apprehensively. He's as quick as a whip with numbers, a perfectionist; engineers are

trained to be accurate and precise. He is dressed simply, in black jeans and a plain semi-casual short-sleeved shirt. I do not suspect him.

My eyes wander about until my gaze stops on a man named Edward. Edward, Phoebe's father, is consoling and reassuring her that there is nothing to fear. He is a regal man, being exceptionally rich, almost as rich as the Huit family. Although he is only in his late forties, his expensive attire makes him appear substantially wiser and older. He looks nearly fifty-five in this particular outfit, mostly because of the expensive, antique gold watch that hangs by a chain from his pocket.

Phoebe, being epileptic, had frequent seizures which affected her memory. It is unfortunate she also suffers from schizophrenia. Her eyes are unforgettable and haunting. She stares into the sky as one whose mind is at peace, analogous to total serenity. But it was so much more than that… I was straying from my purpose. I need to focus on the process of finding the killer and the suspects. I think to myself: these two individuals are not suspects.

Edgar's mother-in-law flips tediously through files of a law report. Mysteriously, no one knows her first name. Everyone refers to her as Mrs. Logan or as Rachel's mother. She is a stern lady and certainly someone to be avoided — definitely not a people person and clearly not easy to be around. She is the complete opposite of Rachel. The thought of Mrs. Logan gives me chills and turns me off. She is indeed pleasantly dressed and rich without a doubt. My instincts tell me to delve deeper into her character and actions.

There isn't much to say about Rachel — honest, no nonsense, and to the point. She is not the killer. Instead, my attention focuses on her mother. I need to find out all I can about Mrs. Logan. She is, above all others, fuelling my suspicions. My instincts guide me to look at her more closely.

I slowly make my way over to Mrs. Logan, to ask for her first name, but Stacey abruptly stops me. She asks me with a mean stare, "Now what are you going to do? Oh right, let's go and jump to conclusions again."

"Of course not!" I chuckle. "I am just going to ask for some water." I continue walking.

"I'm right, aren't I?"

"You read me like a book…"

"You're thirsty?" She held out a bottle of mineral water and smiles innocently. I smile and turn towards the stained glass

window. The snow is accumulating quickly and soon it turns into a full-fledged blizzard. On the radio, the broadcaster announces storm warnings stating that it will limit travel and seriously impact large areas. I head over to the entrance door, unlock it, and try to push it open, but it is futile. It is just as I expect... We are snowed in.

"Oh dear!" Rachel gasps, as she too, understands what happened. "I assume everyone will be staying the night. No problem. There's enough room to accommodate everyone here," she smiles hospitably.

Mrs. Logan heads for the washroom. I glide quickly towards Mrs. Logan before she makes it to the door. "Excuse my rudeness and my abruptness, but I want to know your first name?"

She stares at me, "Well, a young man like you should know when, or rather when not to, question people."

I look at her in bewilderment.

"What I mean to say is..." She pauses as if her response is the most anticipated moment of the evening.

"Mind your own damn business!" She shoves me forcefully aside and enters the washroom, slamming the door firmly shut.

What a rude and odd person she is. I wondered why she wouldn't give her first name? What keeps her from doing so? Her actions just reinforce my suspicion of her as the lead suspect, the murderer.

An excerpt from the novel
STUCK IN WONDERLAND
by Christina Clapperton

DESPITE FEELING FRUSTRATED AND distracted that afternoon, I attempted to help prepare a five-course meal for Greaves' party.

"It's too bad about the timing with what happened at work. It's too late to cancel, but you don't have to be here. I can book you a room at the King Eddy. That way you can go to sleep when you want to."

"No. I'll be fine, Mom. Thanks."

The place filled up quickly. Like the parties she attended, it was formal: dresses and heels and suits, even ties. Greaves opened the French doors so that the overflow from the dining room could move into the kitchen. Looking down at herself, she gasped. "I've been serving hors d'oeuvres with this ridiculous apron on." She laughed and shook her head.

"I don't know why I didn't notice," I said, untying her apron covered in bright red, orange, and yellow tomatoes. She was now clad in a long, black fitted dress, another one of her classic, understated pieces. I preferred a more casual look but admired how she put so much care into her wardrobe and made it look effortless.

Only the highest quality of fabrics, perfectly tailored.

I said hello as I passed my aunts Mya and Gail, Greaves' sisters. Near the entrance where I hung up the apron stood a tall, slim woman in a green dress with red hair piled on the top of her head. There was something about the green and the red and the way she leaned in to speak over the brassy jazz music that made her look like a long-stemmed rose swaying in the breeze.

I checked to see if Greaves needed any help getting dinner ready. She said she was fine and that I should go mingle. I felt more comfortable parking myself next to Claire, a close friend of hers, enveloped in magenta satin like cellophane-wrapped candy.

"Free food turns the city's most respected into savages doesn't it?" remarked Claire. Even though Claire was no longer jetting off to the Milan and Paris runways, I felt like a bit of a celebrity standing beside her. I was embarrassed to have only recently found out that Botox, not the face creams Claire endorsed, had turned her back into a twenty-two-year-old Barbie doll. "It's always the lesser-knowns who arrive early," she continued when I didn't respond. "They spare nothing but the white doilies. You'd think they only eat when they don't have to pay for the food. Actually, I should take that back. I wouldn't say all of them are respected. We do have a politician in the room."

"Who?"

"That one over there." With one finger of the hand holding her wine glass, she pointed in the direction of a middle-aged man in a blue-grey suit that was more fashion-forward than I expected of a politician. His pocket square was in a contrasting pattern to the wide tie that lay over the extended girth of his abdomen. Just then he laughed, thrusting his stomach further forward, nearly spilling his scotch. "He ran for mayor in the last election. Or the one before that."

Greaves was starting to serve dinner. I hooked Claire's arm and nodded at the dining room table. The people congregating at the kitchen island looked like professor types or arrogant businessmen. I noticed a worried look on my aunt Gail's face when we took the last seats in the dining room. She and Mya would have to sit at the kitchen island. Gail would much rather Mya talk to people she knew. She got embarrassed easily when Mya discussed her job.

I thought Mya always managed to talk about it in a twisted way that made just about anyone nod in understanding. Mya liked the fancy parties high-profile clients took her to. And she'd say,

"Every evening is like a psychology class. You learn so much about what goes on in peoples' minds." But I always flinch when she'd say she enjoyed how the job allowed her to meet different kinds of people. Sure, I could agree that there are a lot of interesting people to meet in this world, but their turn-ons and fetishes were not exactly ways in which I was inclined to get to know them.

I couldn't hear much of what Mya and Gail were talking about during dinner but I could tell Gail was dominating the conversation. Mya looked annoyed, and I bet it was because Gail was cutting her off when people asked her questions. Mya had told her once, when she had enough of her judgment, that she couldn't understand how what she did was any less socially acceptable than Gail letting her children be raised by teachers in Switzerland.

Mya never saw her daughter Tanya. But if Tanya were interested, Mya said she would welcome her back to live with her, even though she was now in her late twenties. Gail wanted time to herself but enjoyed seeing her children during the summer and winter holidays. I could appreciate how difficult it would be to raise a nine- and an eleven-year-old virtually on her own with the father being out-of-town so frequently, but I had a feeling that if they were mine, I would miss them too much if they were so far away.

After dinner, Gail edged Mya over to the kitchen where Claire and I were drinking chilled sauterne and sampling soft cheeses. Unpasteurized, apparently, was the way to go.

"So, your mother tells me you've quit your job," Gail said.

"Good for you, Mannis," Mya said, louder than necessary, even with the music and competing conversations. At that point, I thought it would have been wise to have kept track of the number of drinks Mya had since the start of the evening.

"Working for a corporation not for you?" Gail said.

"You know, I think it's really sad how people stay in stressful jobs they don't like. If they leave, they seem to find other jobs that turn out to be just as bad. Can't they see they're repeating the same pattern?"

"Einstein said insanity is doing the same thing over and over again and expecting different results," Gail said in a jaunty tone.

"A lot of people talk about getting out and owning their own business, but not many can give up their security," I said.

"It looks like the only problem is that you've outsmarted yourself from the opportunity to be content in a job with a regular paycheque," Gail said, only partially joking I'm sure.

"The paycheque isn't worth it if you don't enjoy what you do," I said. I wasn't oblivious of her point. I knew people who lacked finances and how stressful that is. I had no doubt that leaving a job would be an even more difficult decision to make if children are involved. Some jobs were necessary and someone would have to do them, but I didn't want it to be me, or anyone I cared about if it made them unhappy.

"You know, modelling can be like having your own business if you do it without an agent. They don't take them as thick as you for runway, but you have the perfect hourglass figure for lingerie," Claire said.

Claire was too caught up in lending her opinion to consider that I might be bothered by her harsh comment. While she went on, for a second I pictured myself posing next to Claire in a pink lace bra and panty. I would coyly turn my head to the side without moving my eyes and thrust my hips back, making my butt look higher and as soft and round as a poached plum. "Thanks, Claire, but I'm not interested in modelling."

"I guess you don't want to hear my suggestion then," Mya said, no doubt hoping for an enthusiastic response.

"You're not going to get Mannis involved in any of that," Greaves said, out of nowhere while making rounds to refill glasses.

"Like the only thing stopping me from joining Mya tomorrow night is your prohibition," I said.

"That's not what I was referring to," Mya said to Greaves. "Cachet has other clients with different needs. I don't do it because the work is irregular. My regulars keep me busy, and you know how much I love my regulars."

"Yes, Mya, we all know how much you love your job," Greaves said.

"Cachet needs hostesses strictly to accompany men at parties."

"Forget it," Greaves said, pinning her eyes on Mya.

"Okay, fine."

"You know, that gave me an idea," Claire said.

"Claire, I appreciate that you want to help, but I don't think an idea spawned from hostessing is up my alley."

Greaves gave me the "good one" look.

"No, I mean things like car shows; golf courses hire girls to hand out prizes for the best putt."

"That's modelling," I exclaimed. "I know you mean well,

Claire. I understand that it works for you, but that doesn't mean it would work for me. I just have too much enmity towards the fashion and modelling industries for making adolescent girls think that their tiny, undeveloped bodies have expanded outside the borders of acceptability. And don't get me started on the advertising industry that capitalizes on it with ads for everything from face creams to diet pills that promise to change who we are, because we're just not good enough."

"Well put," Claire said, after a few moments contemplating my comment that put down the industry she has been in for three decades. Claire knew that I loved her. We were known to have our debates.

All the talk about work, whether inadvertent or my doing, ended the night for me pretty early. I took the boa Mya had given me out of my closet. Sitting on my bed, I wrapped it around me. Would it be so bad being a hostess? The money doing practically anything else wouldn't come close. I could see a wealthy businessman calling up Cachet to send him a young, attractive, wholesome-looking woman for a date. No sex required. He would be handsome. He just hasn't had any luck with women. They all want his money or become jealous when he's anywhere near another woman. He doesn't want to come to the party dateless.

I pictured myself in a cab, asking the driver to stop a block away from the party so we could walk in together arm-in-arm. On the walk over, we'd get our stories straight. Co-conspirators, actors. Incredibly exciting. I would wear a strapless sequin-embroidered gown. Men all around me would observe the glowing lights dancing on my bare shoulders. To make it look realistic, he would put his arm around me but keep it a professional two inches above my backside. That's fine. I could handle that.

He would introduce me to his friends who tell him I must be blind. It becomes a running joke throughout the night as I charm them with my grace and intelligent conversation. "Are you sure she didn't sustain a head injury?" the friends say. He would put his arm around me again, but this time he's had a few drinks, and my butt cheek is resting in the curve of his hand. I would excuse myself to the powder room. But before I wriggle out of his grip, he'd give me a full kiss on my lips. Forget it. Never. Not in this lifetime.

I PICTURE MYSELF AT THAT MOMENT
by Nancy Kay Clark

I COME FROM A long line of sales people and hypochondriacs.
My sister is a peri-menopausal, lactose-intolerant, software sales rep
with an irritable bowel. She often wakes up with mysterious rashes.
Kath came to visit me in the hospital today. She perched on my bed
and lifted her shirt to reveal a spread of blotches around her middle.
"Do you think this is shingles? Will they start oozing if I scratch
them?"

"Don't scratch them, then."

"But is it shingles?"

"I have no idea. Do they hurt?"

"No."

"I think shingles is supposed to hurt."

"Maybe I should ask your nurse."

"Don't ask the nurse."

"Why the hell not?"

"Please don't ask the nurse."

She asked the nurse.

After that, James arrived bearing gifts. He gave me three old
copies of *The New Yorker* and a notebook, which he called a health

journal. The cover is pink and purple paisley. He bought it so that I can write down all my questions for the doctors, note their answers, jot down my hourly blood sugar levels and paste in all their business cards. He says he'll buy me a binder so that I can organize all the info I find on the Internet about my perilous condition. He says I should keep it always at hand — no doubt for pleasant bedtime reading. There's no fucking way I'm researching my condition on the Net. And if he nags me one more time about my cholesterol levels, I'm pitching my Jell-O at him.

He shook his head at me and said with that damn smile of his, "Now Sandra, you're not yourself. You've been through a trauma. I won't stay long. I don't want to over-tax you. You should rest."

James thinks that if he just waits long enough I'll change my mind. *Pontificating ass. Butt-kissing turd. Self-righteous, lip-trembling, psycho-babbling liar.* Since I can still pick up a pen and write, I've decided to use my pink and purple health journal to swear at him.

My cardiologist tells me I have a hole in my heart. After four days in the hospital, gobs of blood tests (I have the arms of a junkie), two MRIs, a CAT scan, an ultrasound and an echocardiogram, they found out my stroke had nothing to do with me being diabetic — because I'm not. And it had nothing to do with my cholesterol levels or blood pressure (which are fine), or the occasional smoke I sneak at faculty parties. It was because I have a hole in my heart. Dr. Neumann tells me it's called a PFO. It's a floppy valve, between the right and left atriums. It opens under pressure — like when you're bearing down to deliver a child or coughing or blowing a gasket.

Essentially, I got so pissed off at James that the hole opened; a blood clot went through the wrong way, travelled up to my brain and then exploded. I picture myself as a cartoon character with a bright red face and steam coming out of my ears. Now, every time I cough or sneeze or laugh hard my right hand goes up to my chest, as if to hold the flap door closed.

Kath was with me when Dr. Neumann told me about my PFO. She asked him whether heart holes are hereditary. She's decided she has one too.

Apparently fifteen percent of us have this type of hole. I wonder if it expands or contracts depending on how cold it is outside? Was it open or closed when I was five and my cat Celia got run over by that truck? Or when I was ten and dad moved out? Or when I was a grad student and first met James, sitting by himself in

the corner of the coffee shop drinking mint tea?

Late in the afternoon, my baby brother Tom showed up. He kissed me on the forehead and tossed me a couple of Harlequin romances, which he had rummaged from his wife's bedside table. "I know you like these things, Sandi."

I looked at the dog-eared paperbacks. The one with the pirate was called *Heart of No Return*. The cowboy one was called *The Patchwork Wife*. Tom grinned. "I marked the sex scenes for you."

I grinned back — sort of — my left side still sags. I told Tom that some of my brain cells were now dead — that I was officially brain damaged. He didn't seem surprised. "Oh, I thought that happened in high school. Where's Kath?"

I shrugged. "She went to ask about booking an echocardiogram."

"For you?"

"For herself."

He didn't comment on that, instead he asked me how James was. I told him that as soon as I get out of here, I'm kicking that marathon-running clean freak out of the house. Tom nodded and then squeezed his two hundred and fifty-pound frame into the vinyl-covered chair at the foot of my bed. He told me about his new flat-screen TV. I asked about his sinus troubles. After a while, he went off to inspect the washrooms. Tom sells wall-mounted hand dryers and soap dispensers for a living.

Last Friday, during the monthly luncheon meeting of the National Council of Statistical Analysts, Toronto Chapter, James was giving a speech on Rasch Measurement. I was sitting beside a woman I had just met — a new member — her name was Sylvia, I think. James was talking about estimating maximum likelihoods, when I noticed that the jacket of my pinstriped suit was covered in wet splotches. I was crying, and not just a little bit. My shoulders heaved. Sylvia turned my chair sideways, facing hers, so that the men at our table wouldn't see. She pressed Kleenex into my hands. She didn't ask me what was wrong, which was good, because I'm not sure I could have told her.

It was just that…it was that stupid speech. His point-form notes on his little cue cards, all neatly printed. His PowerPoint presentation with the multi-coloured pie charts and bar graphs. His perfect intonation and delivery. He rehearsed that speech about fifty times at night.

It was me who sat there. I'm the one who listened. I'm

the one who had to make intelligent comments. I'm the one who went to all those luncheon meetings and conferences. And when an audience was lukewarm, I'm the one who whispered in his ear, "No, no, you did good. You did good." Every night, I patched him up and every morning I sent him off, telling him to go out there and conquer the world. Instead he goes out and does the brunette from the next cubicle over.

After the luncheon, we were walking along Dundas Street, back to our cars. By then my eyes were dry and I told James I wanted him out.

"But it happened months ago!" he said.

"Well, I've been thinking about it for a while."

"But I thought we had agreed that you would forgive me."

"No, I said that I would try to forgive you. There's a difference."

When I first found out about the brunette, I called Kath. I tried to explain it.

"He said it was her brain, her brilliant brain he was drawn to."

Kath snorted. Then she told me how she had caught one of her old boyfriends cheating on her with three other women at the same time. "That's just way worse than James. You've got to admit, Sandi, I've had much shittier boyfriends than you."

"Yes," I replied. "I've been lucky."

It was right after I asked James to move out. While he was puffing away about how unfair I was being, the hole in my heart opened wide and the clot reached my brain. There was a whirl and a tilt and a laser light show. James kept talking, but I was waiting for the world to stop shifting and I forgot to listen. Then I was sprawled on the sidewalk, nylons ripped, power skirt scrunched up, and I kept saying, "I feel weird, I feel weird" — except it didn't come out that way, because by this time I was slurring my words.

James told me to sit up. I tried. I told my brain to tell my body to sit up, but my brain was exploding and didn't answer. I lay there on the sidewalk and felt something heavy pressing on my chest. A dead weight. I couldn't budge it. It turns out it was my left arm.

I'll be in the hospital for another couple of days, while I arrange for some home care and weekly physio. James offered to drive me to the condo, but I told him that Tom would. I told James not to be there when I arrived.

This morning in the hospital I found myself stuck in the toilet. It's that damn left leg. I rang and rang the bell, but no one came. I waited and then Kath showed up for her daily visit and found me. She went to get help as I sat there, on the sticky floor, eye to eye with the rinsed out bedpans. They came quickly after that, helped me stand and got me back into bed. Kath whispered to me, "I told them off for you. They said the bell must not be working, but I think they're full of shit."

I laughed hard and brought my hand to my chest.

THE PATH TO TRANSFORMATION AND FORGIVENESS
by Juliet Davy

A Child's Dream

HERE I AM, STROLLING in the park, pondering over and over in my busy mind. Where and how do I start my story? The pain that I feel inside is deep. My heart and soul yearns for answers. Why are we so separated? Why can't there be love and unity among my brothers and sisters? Why do children have to suffer the consequence of the past generation? My life is built on oppression, persecution, and crisis. I see my family in torment, hardship, mental slavery, and self sabotage.

I spend my entire journey searching for answers. The big questions: Why me? Why my family?

Then I blame you mom.

It's your fault mom.

You brought us into this world, you should protect us, mom.

You should provide for us in a better way, mom.

I blame you for all the hardship!

Mom, as I see you now, the warrior, broken-hearted, scared,

guilty, and wondering why you, the light is turned on and we are all asking the same question. "Why me?"

It is sunrise and I wake up. I ask for your forgiveness, mom. I see you did the best you can. You fed us, provided shelter, disciplined us with physical abuse, verbal abuse, emotional abuse, but you did the best you could - a warrior fighting very hard to survive. This is all you know. This is your best.

Forgive me, mom, now my soul is free. Free from the oppression, the persecution, the crises, and abuse. I can see this was you, loving us your way.

I am responsible for me, loving my way.

I forgive you mom.

I love you mom. I love you unconditionally. I hope my love transforms your spirit and frees your soul — frees you from the guilt and mental slavery. May your spirit soar, a warrior, an eagle!

Charlotte And Hope

Charlotte, strong, beautiful, black warrior from the Maroon tribe, with a complexion of olive, hair thick, woollen but with the feel of silk, and with the eyes of an eagle, stands majestically on the peak of Blue Mountain.

Far below, Hope strolls through the park unaware of the heat and the humidity. Hope, with a calm personality, and compassion, constantly seeks the truth. Her aura is like the blue lagoon.

Hope, blown by the wind of the south to a country now called home, gives birth to two beautiful children. Her first born, a daughter, she gives up, choosing to keep her little boy. Surely this sacrifice would give her the opportunity to get a good education and a better life? Her mind races with confusion.

Charlotte, a warrior mother of six beautiful children, forced to come down from her sanctuary to a world she could not cope with, struggles to adjust to the unknown and uncivilized in her new world. Being illiterate poses quite a challenge for Charlotte in her new life. In her sanctuary, wisdom is more a way of life. Charlotte survives using her intuition and her deep inner strength that had made her a true warrior.

Hope burdened with her family pain and separation misses her brother and sisters. Confused, she needs answers to her questions. 'How can I unite my family? Why are my brothers and sisters separated? How can I create peace and love between

my siblings? Why do children suffer the consequences of the past generations?' Angry and frustrated, she blames her mother for the family dysfunctions.

Hope begins her journey and as if from nowhere a light goes on in Hope's dream. She is awake. Hope sees her entrapment in the pattern of generational struggle and with all her inner strength and persistence, she breaks the pattern. She reclaims the child she gave up. She is a loving mother of her son, teaches children in a public school and finds herself in the performing arts. But, is this is all a dream?

Hope sees her shadow in Charlotte's journey. Asking Charlotte for forgiveness, she spread her wings and screams, "I am free."

The echoes shout back at her,
"I am free! I am free!"

PEACHES AND CREMA
by Susan Desveaux

IT WAS JUST LIKE in the movies. The dark sedan moved silently down the driveway. Two grim-faced men in dark suits and Ray Bans got out of the car. As they reached the heavy wooden door, it opened and Jean stood in the entrance, holding a cappuccino.

"Mrs. Martin. Federal Agents." He flashed a badge. "I'm Agent Greene. This is Agent Ross. We'd like to speak to your nephew."

"I have several, but only one who isn't a complete fool," she said to Greene. She was not tall, but at 70, she had mastered the ability to fill the doorway with her body. "If you're referring to Dr. Jean-Gerard Ryan, he comes down here on weekends when he can get away. I believe he's away on business at the moment." Her tone was crisp. In the past it would have withered a young person, but at 70, her withering capability had diminished.

"Dr. Ryan has not been at work for the past three days and there is no record of any trips scheduled through Luridon Pharmaceuticals. The company is, naturally, concerned. Since he was working on a government-sponsored project ..." He left the doom and gloom hanging in the air and paused. "May we come

in?" The question was a formality. He handed her a search warrant and after a dozen heartbeats, she stood aside.

"My refusing wouldn't stop you. Keep in mind this is a healing centre. Try not to mess it up."

They walked into her living room where three women in their late seventies, dressed in yoga sweats, lay on their backs, necks extended, spines arched. Jean cleared her throat and the women sat up, turning toward the door in unison.

"Goodness, Jean," Martha said. "I didn't know we were expanding the class. Should I make some more cappuccino?"

"They're Feds, looking for JG. They can get their own cappuccino when they leave."

"Feds!" said Jessie. "Are you sure? Did you see a badge? Do they have a warrant?"

"They come fully equipped." Jean replied grimly, waving the warrant.

The living room was very large, with enough space for a yoga class. On the coffee table sat a plate of fruit tarts and three cups of cappuccino. A coral-coloured cockatiel perched in a corner next to an ornate glass-doored armoire filled with antique chinoiserie. He was eating a grape. Sunflower seeds fanned out over the floor under his perch. The room was lined with bookcases; a library of art, music, alternative health, and spiritual books. One bookshelf stored a large collection of vinyl records, CDs of chants and sacred music, and an ancient stereo system.

The agents stood in the doorway scanning the room with their eyes and began to search, rifling through Jean's desk, ruffling the papers, looking through the bills and examining her bank book. Ross searched the bedrooms. They looked through the medicine chests in the bathrooms, taking time to examine the prescription bottles and the over-the-counter meds, taking the lids off the shampoos and sniffing.

When they returned to the living room, Ross's eyes fell on the computer that sat on the ledge of the pass-through window into the kitchen.

"Does Dr. Ryan ever use this computer?" Ross was already in the kitchen and booting up the elderly Mac. Earlier in the day, someone had been baking peach tarts, peach pies and making peach preserves. The room smelled of peaches and orange and ginger. Jean followed him at a distance.

"Certainly not," she said. "JG always travels with his own

laptop."

"Peaches," the bird said and dipped its head into the bowl. It delicately removed a piece of peach from the bowl and ate it. Ross was working his way through the files on the hard drive. The bird ruffled its feathers, stretched its wings. "Peaches," it said again, and threw a piece of soft, ripe peach into the pass-through, hitting Ross on the head. Ross glared at the bird and kept working.

"Nothing," he said bitterly. "No erasures, no steganography … nada."

"I'm afraid, all you're going to find on that is my recipe collection." Jean was watching them intently, but she might as well have been invisible. "Well, unless you want my top-secret recipe for peach jam, or want to tell the world how much money I have in my account, or you're moonlighting for Martha Stewart, are you quite through?"

Greene drew her to one side. It was clear to Jean that he was preparing to show his earnest and concerned side.

"Mrs. Martin, your nephew is missing. Right now, we don't know if he's taking a few days off or whether he has been kidnapped. This is very serious. Has he spoken to you about his work?"

"Something to do with cows," Jessie said, smiling beatifically. "He always liked animals."

"Cows?" Greene said.

"Mrs. Wilson is a little confused," Jean interjected. "JG is a neuroscientist. He's working toward a cure for variant Creutzfeldt-Jakob disease, the human form of 'mad cow' disease."

"Initially, that may have been the case. Are you aware that Dr. Ryan's research interest has evolved into a study of the basic nature of intelligence?"

"JG believed that there was a serious lack of intelligence in some quarters of the world … mostly in government," Jean replied wryly. "He always said, 'If you could bottle brains, politicians should be force-fed."

"Are you aware that he may have succeeded?" Greene continued. "We believe Dr. Ryan has discovered a substance, a drug or hormone of some kind that enhances intelligence." He paused for a moment. "You can see how important that is … how a foreign government might want that secret." He let the implication hang in the air.

"I don't see how any government, particularly this one, could be interested in intelligence," Martha shot back from the couch.

"Nevertheless," Greene replied, directing his attention to Jean, "If you hear from him, he must get in touch with us. If you know where he keeps his notes, any computer discs, we need to have them."

"Are you telling me that JG has disappeared with all of his research notes and experimental data on this discovery ...?" Jean's voice trailed off.

"The facts bear that interpretation." Greene said and followed Ross out. Turning at the door, he played the trump card. "It would be in your best interest to help us. You could be a target for persons wanting to find your nephew." She took the card without a word.

The agents got into their car and drove away. The ladies sat around the kitchen table, drank cappuccino, ate tarts, and waited.

"The worst combination of *The Matrix, Men in Black* and *Get Smart,*" Jessie said, shaking her head.

"Do you think it's safe to continue?" Martha asked. "Should we sweep the place for bugs?"

"I don't think so. The phone is probably tapped in case JG calls, as if he would be so stupid," Jean replied. "JG was always a bright man... even before he made himself the first human trial subject of Crema. He wouldn't fall for anything so obvious."

"Well, if you're sure..." Martha was unconvinced.

"Bureaucrats have no imagination. We're old ladies. They think we're disposable, unworthy of consideration," Jean replied. "And I have a few tricks up my sleeve. I think taking Crema not only enhances intelligence, it makes you crafty. I know I feel like I could play chess with the world."

"I know what you mean," Jessie laughed. "I think my grandkids are beginning to get suspicious... but my daughter is completely oblivious." They smiled at each other.

"All right, Emily, let's begin." Jean began to take charge. The intrusion of the agents had unsettled her and she wanted to get the treatment over with. "Has everyone finished their cappuccino? The vascular effect of the caffeine is very important." The ladies put their cups in the sink. "And the tarts. Don't forget to maximize your fructose, it moves the Crema into the brain more quickly."

Emily settled herself back on the yoga mat and attempted the Fish asana. Jessie and Martha propped her into the correct position. Jean moved in behind the cockatiel and opened the armoire. Inside, amongst the chinoiseri was a very old lacquer apothecary's box. She took a key from around her neck and opened the box. Inside were

small glassine envelopes filled with white powder, a box of vials of sterile saline solution and a small nasal spray bottle. Jean quickly poured the contents of one envelope and one vial into the spray bottle and began swirling it around to mix the contents.

"Are you sure you can't do this?" Emily asked as Jean knelt down and handed her the spray bottle. "It's so awkward."

"Of course I could, my dear. I'm a doctor, Jean said. "But JG was very specific. You self-administer Crema. It's your way of consenting, and it protects the rest of us. And anyway, this is your first dose, you should enjoy it."

Emily sighed. "Yoga is very uncomfortable." She took the bottle and sprayed the solution into her nose, three sprays on each side until all the solution was gone.

"I know," said Jean. "But the Fish position is the ideal one to get the solution into those little blood vessels in the nose and a direct line into the brain."

After a few minutes Emily sat up, and then stood. She stretched her arms over her head. "I feel wonderful. Like I just had a big glass of champagne … all bubbles and lightness." She sat on the sofa next to Martha.

"That's the 'Crema' effect," Jean said, "like the creamy foam that rises up and covers the surface of espresso and cappuccino. JG's Crema allows new neural pathways to form and boosts the capabilities of the human mind, like intelligence floating to the surface of the brain."

While they were talking and making more cappuccino, Jean took out a ledger with "Yoga Fitness" printed on the cover. She made some brief notes about Emily's experience and then tucked it back into the bottom drawer of her desk.

"What are we doing today—astronomy—space recognition—differential calculus?"

Martha and Jessie were eager to exercise their minds with esoteric subjects. Jean placed some pads and pens in front of her friends, and looked at them with more pride and love than she had ever felt for anyone except JG. Martha, who had started sliding into despair after Alec's death, had rekindled her love for the law; Jessie whose memory had been failing and who feared Alzheimer's more than any other shadow, was deeply involved in forensic sciences.

Jean was proud of their courage. When they volunteered to be the third and fourth human trials of the intelligence-enhancing Crema, Jean had been concerned. Although she and JG had

experienced no negative side effects from Crema, there were no guarantees — but her friends were not afraid. They were blossoming with more vitality than ever before — and now Emily had joined the circle.

"Einstein," Jean said, looking at the corner. "What's next in the protocol?"

"The next protocol involves three dimensional chess with a Grandmaster computer program," the cockatiel said. "I would suggest we put that aside for the moment."

"You're worried, now that the feds have started sniffing around," Jean replied.

"I think we need to develop an escape plan," Einstein said, ruffling his feathers. "If they find JG, he won't be able to hold out forever. They'll eventually get the formula out of him. Since I'm the only other one with the formula and protocols, you and I need to be prepared. Agent Greene is not as dim as he looks. He'll be back. I don't think you ladies can count on hiding your brains for too much longer. There's nothing more lethal than brains and experience." The bird scratched the side of his head with a toe. "And by the way, I'm sick of peaches."

SPONTANEOUS ADVENTURE
by Sally Dillon

ON THE NIGHT OF April 9th, 1955 when I was fifteen, I stood at a neighbour's home and watched, out of their living room window, the large red flames jut up and rush into the dark sky. My home on Bondhead Street burned to the ground as I watched helplessly. It was 7:30 pm.

An hour earlier, I left my home to go across the street to the neighbour's home to babysit their children. I settled the children down peacefully in their beds for the night, picked up a magazine to read, and curled into their comfortable easy chair. Suddenly, a loud banging on the back door and my younger sister's voice shouting, "Sally, Sally our house is on fire," brought me back from the world of the magazine. I flung the door wide open and asked my sister if everyone was out of the home. "Yes," she said. I immediately telephoned the Trenton Fire Department and gave the municipal address of my home. The fireman on the other end of the line asked me to repeat the address and to give the nearest major intersection or major building close to my home. I told him it was very close to the Allore Lumber yard. The fireman said they would be on their way.

Eight minutes later, with the whirling sound of the sirens, the large fire engines pulled up to the barn-like structure that was my home. The firemen lugged their huge hoses off the truck. The whoosh sound of the water gushing from their hoses could be heard as the water hit the large red flames sending black clouds of smoke up into the still April sky. Our family dog, Sparky, could be heard barking inside the burning structure while my fourteen year old brother Robert had to be held back by two policemen to stop him from entering the burning structure to save Sparky.

As I stood there viewing this tragedy from the window, I could see a crowd begin to gather — friends, neighbours, media reporters, and others, came to view this fire out of curiosity. My parents were not at home when the fire erupted and arrived on the scene immediately after hearing the news.

At 9:00 pm the flames had somewhat subsided. I was in a mild state of shock. I thought to myself, "I am only fifteen years old. What will become of me? Where will I go? This must be a bad dream and when I awake everything will be okay." Tears welled in my eyes. I had just lost all of my personal possessions and left with only the clothes I was wearing. After checking with my parents, I accepted the invitation from my neighbour where I was babysitting, to spend the rest of the night on their sofa.

Before falling asleep I thought of the fire and of what I had lost — my baby precious doll that had been on my bed for so many years and our family pet dog Sparky… I said my prayers to my creator and thanked him for sparing my family of four brothers, three sisters and my parents.

I was born in that house on August 11, 1940. One sister and two brothers had arrived in that home before me. Trenton did not have a hospital at that time, so expectant mothers had to travel to Belleville to have their babies. We did not have a family car and could not afford the expense of the hospital stay so my mother had all of her babies at home with the assistance of Dr. J. V. Byrne and his nurse who we called Nurse Hazlem. This was the time of World War II and people dressed their children in air force and navy uniforms, saying, "Don't they look cute?" My late grandparents owned the large white house on the corner of Front and Bondhead Streets, now a used car lot. My father had (with the help of architects and friends) built our home at the rear of my grandparents' lot and it became municipally known as 18 Bondhead Street.

The morning following the fire, our homeless family gathered

at the home of my Aunt Florence Gannon, my father's sister, for a family meeting. They decided that, for the time being and until future living quarters were obtained, our family would have to split up. My parents, my younger brother and two sisters would stay with my Aunt Florence. My older brothers, sisters and I would be accommodated at the homes of our closest friends. I chose to stay with my two classmates and their single Dad in an apartment close to downtown Trenton, near my school, St. Peter's Roman Catholic School. I was in grade nine.

After having eaten a nutritious lunch at the home of my Aunt Florence, my father asked me if I wanted to accompany him to our former home, which now lay in shambles. I accepted and the two of us walked over to investigate what was left of our personal belongings. I told my Dad that there was a $10.00 bill in my jeans pocket which was given to me as an Easter gift by a friend. The two of us walked up the charcoal charred steps being very careful not to fall and entered into what was left of my former bedroom. I found the jeans badly water damaged on the floor. I inserted my hand into the pocket and pulled out the $10.00 bill. I was thrilled that it was still in one piece. I gave it to my father. I could see by the expression on his face that he was very, very sad and thought that this would cheer him up.

A while later my father and I stood on the sidewalk staring at the ruins of the home that had been a major part of our lives. I will always keep in my heart the words my father uttered to me on that bright April day. He said, "Sally, remember this day and what I am about to tell you. It is not what we have lost that counts, it is what we do with what we have left." I ate those words up and swallowed them. They remained with me throughout my life and it has come in handy when I have had to pick myself up, dust myself off, and start all over again in order to obtain much better circumstances within a situation.

As I stood there on that sidewalk I thought to myself, "What is going to become of our close knit family now? Will we still be as close as we once were? What will happen to me? Will my classmates at school still treat me the same as they had prior to the fire?" I felt sad.

I later discovered that my older sister Rita, who was then twenty-four years old, was sleeping in her upstairs bedroom when the fire broke out. My younger sister Norah, eleven years old at the time, ran upstairs to awaken Rita, and then guided her down

the smoky stairs and out the front door to the city sidewalk. I call this a remarkable act of bravery on Norah's part. I also learned that the fire had started on the second floor of the home where the stove pipes had become so red hot that they had burst. A brand new oil furnace had been installed just one month earlier. My fourteen year old brother Robert had been babysitting my younger brother and two younger sisters at the time, while my older sister Rita was in her bedroom. They had not been instructed to turn the damper down on the new oil furnace. The damper was located sticking out from the stovepipe downstairs.

At the time the fire broke out, my Dad was at the local pub with some of his friends and my Mom was playing bingo at the local bingo hall. My eldest brother James was working his usual shift at the pool hall downtown, and my second oldest brother Andrew was at the movies.

My first day at my grade nine class after the fire held a pleasant surprise. All of the students in my class were kind to me as well as sympathetic about my loss. Staying with my two girlfriends was fun. I now had a remarkable sense of freedom while living there. There was no supervision. The girl's father was at work from 10:00 am until 7:00 pm. Their mother had passed away five years earlier. We all had the responsibility of keeping the apartment clean as well as doing our own laundry, dishes and shopping. The three of us shared a large bedroom on the upper floor of the apartment while the girl's father occupied a bedroom on the main floor of the apartment. These two friends became as close to me as my sisters for many, many years to come.

The second day of school after the fire, as I entered my grade nine classroom, I found to my surprise that there was a personal shower of gifts waiting for me from my classmates. The gifts consisted of items of clothing as well as personal packages for use in my activities of daily living. Needless to say, I greatly appreciated this gesture and was at a loss for words and in my shyness I just said "thanks" to the class as a whole. I asked myself, "would my life ever be the same as it was while I lived in my former home?" The answer had to be "No."

A CULINARY CONNECTION
by Graham Ducker

IT WAS NEARLY TIME to open and I was worried. I was concerned for two connected reasons: yesterday my master chef, Henri, had buried his grandmother who raised him from infancy; and I was apprehensive that the entrees at The West Bank Experience, Fine French Cuisine, might not be up to standard.

At four o'clock I unlocked the main door, knowing that most patrons would not arrive until after seven. I glanced into the kitchen. It was obvious my portly and usually jovial cook was hurting as he seemed critical of everything Charles, his apprentice, attempted.

I was about to intercede when a diminutive senior lady entered the foyer.

"Are you open?" she asked.

"Why, yes we are. Won't you come in?"

"I don't know if I should." Her eyes flashed. "It looks expensive." She looked at her hands. "I'm just looking for a place to have a quiet cup of tea."

"We can handle that," I invited. "Are you hungry?"

Multi-ringed fingers tightened on the beaded cloth purse.

"Heaven knows I should be," she started, "But ever since

Phil's funeral I haven't been able to eat a thing. My stomach just knots up, if you know what I mean."

"How long were you married?" I ventured.

There was a tiny chuckle. "Oh my, I've been a widow for years. No, my grandson was killed in a car crash a few days ago and…"

She began rummaging in her handbag.

I snatched a cloth napkin and handed it to her.

After dabbing her eyes she looked up. "I'm sorry. I shouldn't be bothering you with my troubles."

"Not at all," I smiled. Gently taking her elbow, I led her to a small table in an isolated corner. "This will be nice and cozy for you."

I motioned to one of the waiters.

"Would you please bring this lady a pot of tea? I want to talk to Henri."

Leaving her in capable hands, I hurried into the kitchen where I put my arm around Henri's broad shoulders.

"Henri, my friend, how would you like to apply your personal expertise to a very special customer?"

His immaculate mustache twisted in a quizzical look.

"Don't worry about the menu," I assured him. "It will be slow for a while yet and Charles is quite capable of looking after any customers."

Curiosity showed in Henri's face as I led him to the door.

"Come and meet her."

The elderly woman put down her teacup as we approached.

"Henri," I began, "This is…?"

"Mrs. Harrison," she finished. "Doris Harrison."

"Mrs. Harrison, this is Henri, our master chef."

As they shook hands, I addressed Henri. "Mrs. Harrison has not had much of an appetite for the past few days."

I pulled a chair out, indicated for him to sit down, and then I turned to the lady.

"Mrs. Harrison…" I started.

"Doris. Please call me Doris."

"Okay Doris, if anyone can cure a missing appetite, it is Henri. I have to go, but I'll let you explain why you have not been eating."

I patted Henri on the shoulder. "Don't worry about the

kitchen." I then spoke to the staff who agreed to steer customers away this area.

The corner-table drama unfolded. Tentative at first, the two heads soon bent closer. She dabbed her eyes while he patted her hand. Later, she dabbed his eyes and patted his hand.

No one dared to refill the teapot.

I was helping Charles with the devilled lobster canapés when Henri, beaming like a little kid, burst into the kitchen.

"Mon Dieu, she is like my own Grandmere! And she is starving! I shall make for her the perfect dinner – Red Snapper with Lemon Marjoram Butter."

Once again Henri was in fine form.

He was soon brushing marjoram butter over two broiled fillets framed by roasted potatoes and baby carrots.

"Some Chablis Grand Cru would go well, eh?" he winked.

"I'll get it," I laughed.

As I poured their wine, it was obvious the dinner was secondary to the culinary connection. I left the bottle in the ice bucket.

Much later, as I was assisting Charles with the Cauliflower Crostini hors d'oeuvres, Henri strolled in.

"Helas, she has gone," he sighed and wagging his finger he continued, "But you know, I think she will be back."

"Of course," I teased, "she likes your cooking."

Henri remained serious. He took my hand as tears welled in his intense black eyes.

"Thank you, my friend. I shall never forget this."

He continued to hold my hand.

I could only nod, swallow hard, and smile weakly.

Finally he dropped my hand, walked over to Charles and smiled. "So now, mon ami, how are the lobster canapés coming along?"

An excerpt from the novel
HOMECOMING
by Sherry Isaac

LORING PATTED HIS INFANT daughter's tiny back long after she'd let out her last burp. She'd adjusted to formula easily enough but her mother's breast milk was what she needed, not this God-forsaken cow's milk from a can, thickened and sweetened, a poor imitation of what Celia had provided. Loring looked at the bottle with scorn. Naturally shaped nipple my ass. His wife's nipples had been plump and pink and tiny. This nipple was hard and large and made of rubber. He wanted to kick the table that the bottle rested on, but that would have woken his sweet Hannah Jade and she was dozing so peacefully. The quick rhythm of her breathing, the softness of her downy forehead against his lips calmed him.

He'd had them both at home, his happy, healthy family. Celia had slipped into the role of motherhood the way Loring's hand slipped under the folds of her nightgown. Effortlessly. She'd had some bleeding for several weeks after Hannah's birth but that was normal and soon stopped. Nursing and bathing and rocking their child had become a familiar routine. She'd pranced down the stairs one morning while he sat and sipped his coffee. He caught

sight of her and halted his cup in mid-air. She filled out her jeans beautifully. Her figure had returned, complemented by the swell of her breasts before Hannah woke for her morning fill.

Then there was the discomfort whenever she used the washroom. A bladder infection, swiftly dealt with in a trip to the doctor's office. The symptoms receded and life went on. But the infection had not been beaten; it had merely crept up her urinary tract where it had laid in hiding. Then came the fever, the crippling pain, the blood in her urine. By then Loring was in Regina, a weeklong job fitting an old house with a grand sweeping staircase and hardwood floors. Celia toughed it out at home, never said a word to him on their nightly telephone calls, unwilling to leave her precious newborn with a neighbour long enough to make another visit to the doctor, too stubborn and strong-willed to ask for help, or to ask her husband to come home. When he returned that Friday evening, Celia was curled up on the bathroom floor in agony. He carried her, then Hannah, to the car and brought her to the emergency ward in no time at all. Had she sought help at the first sign of trouble, she'd have been fine. Over the days she waited, the infection had travelled to her kidneys and invaded her tender, healing womb. Three days later she was dead.

The only thing clear to him outside of Hannah's needs was his pilfering of the bottle of Jack Daniels. Steve had gone to the liquor store while V arranged for platters of food. V had sent him from the basement with an armload of freshly laundered diapers to fold. It would keep him busy, and keep him out of her hair while she struggled to manage the finer details of her sister's death. Loring had lost his way to the little room he shared with his daughter and wandered into the living room where Steve set up a makeshift bar.

Good old dependable Steve, he had bought a bottle of everything: gin, vodka, rum and even tequila, plus two bottles of Jack. "One for the wake," he said as he set one bottle on the tray with the others. He held up the second bottle for Loring's inspection. "And one for later. I think we'll need it." Loring nodded, numb, and when Steve went in search of his own living wife, Loring lifted the extra bottle and slipped it under the mounds of cloth diapers, found his way down the hall to his sister-in-law's sewing room and tucked it into the basket of remnants under his foldaway cot.

It was a small room made smaller by the unexpected addition of Hannah's crib and the narrow cot where Loring had spent the last five nights since his Celia's death. Sleepless nights made bearable

only by Hannah's waking, fussing and searching for her mother's breast, the rocking as V warmed the bottle, the artificial nursing, the burping and the settling her back to sleep. Then he would lie awake and stare at the dark ceiling until she woke again and gave him a reason to keep on living for that brief hour until her simple needs were satisfied and she slept once more.

It had all been so quick. The days and nights rolled into one and before Loring knew it, the service was over, the prayers said and the hymns sung, Celia's body cremated, while friends and relatives crowded into Steve and Veronica's small house to eat open-faced egg salad sandwiches.

Loring laid Hannah in her crib, pulled the crocheted blanket up to her still suckling chin. Someone from the funeral home had come by a half-hour earlier with the urn. How efficient, this business of death. Already there was nothing left of his wife's body but ashes in a beautiful vase. Veronica had wanted to put it in the living room but he'd said no. He wasn't ready to display her like a souvenir or a memory; a journey he'd once made that was over too soon. He took Celia into the little room with Hannah, so they could be a family again.

He'd sleepwalked through the days following Celia's death. He sat down on the foldaway bed with the decisions he couldn't remember making, the decision to cremate rather than bury, the decision to pick this urn over the others. At the same time he'd picked his own, asked them to deliver it to his home address, where he would keep it until his own time came.

He set Celia's urn on his lap and traced his fingers along the simple pattern, China blue paisley on brilliant white, the one Celia would have chosen, of that he was certain. The base was narrow, becoming fuller at the top, and sealed with a round lid. He cradled it in his arms and wept.

Loring grew suddenly aware of the din of voices rising and falling in the other room. How long had he been here? How long before someone came looking for him? Perhaps they'd assumed he'd drifted off to sleep with Hannah. Sleep. Ah, yes. Sleep, that elusive state.

He wiped his eyes and stood up, resting the urn on his mattress, propped by pillows, and looked around the room. Snug in her crib, Hannah's little face frowned as she dreamed, then smiled, then frowned again, her eyes moving underneath translucent lids. Loring kissed the tip of his finger then gently pressed it to her rosebud

lips. Then he crouched, reached under the cot and withdrew the bottle of Jack. With his other arm he scooped up Celia's urn and tiptoed out of the room and down the hall.

At the back door he stopped short. Had Hannah made a noise? Had she found him out? For a split second all background voices fell away as he listened for his daughter. Nothing. He took another step, laid his hand on the knob and made ready to step outside.

Hannah's cry rose sharp above the din in the living room. He began to turn but heard brisk steps advancing down the hall. Loring ducked into the open coat closet as the footsteps sped past. He peeked past a jacket sleeve to see Celia's sister slip through the door and watched as she lifted his daughter, lovingly tucked in the crook of her arm, watched as V's face lit up, watched as she cooed at his baby girl. V's hips swayed gently back and forth, so similar yet so different from his Celia's. Hannah was in good hands.

The moment V's back was turned, Loring slipped out of the closet and out the door, his wife's urn in one arm, the bottle of Jack in the other.

An excerpt from the memoir
BREAKING THROUGH THE BULL. HOW GOD WORKS
by Manny Johal

I HAD NO IDEA that my life was about to change. People talk about their conversations with God, Jesus or how some other deity entered their life during moments of crisis. I had no hope, desire, or expectation that anything like that would happen to me.

The day began like any other. I reported to my fire watch job that morning and worked alongside welders trying to repair damage done to the sawmill equipment over the week. For a young university student like me, it was a dream job. I made nineteen dollars an hour for hosing down a small area and watching for potential fires. When I watched for fires outside the sawmill, my attention would wander and I would stare into the distance. I would take this time to admire my surroundings on the lucky days we were posted outside.

That Saturday, a perfect blue sky stretched into the distance. The sun in the eastern sky was warm, the rays skimming over my skin. Diamonds danced across the surface of the river. To the north, lush trees fed by the generous spring rain, spanned the horizon. The waterfront view created a sense of tranquility despite the intrusion of the sawmill. I stood on a scaffold that gave me a bird's eye view of my surroundings: the vastness of the mountains, the river, the

oceans, and I, so small. How did my concerns, anxieties, fears, hopes, and needs, fit into all of this? I ponder the majesty of the mountains and river before me, while an unmistakable distress occupies my mind. Anxiety wells up inside me, consuming me, hollowing out my chest and emptying my stomach. My heart racing, my breathing rapid, I push back tears. All of this before me, and I don't even deserve to be here, I think. I don't deserve this existence or this experience. I wish to disappear.

With a sense of emptiness and despair filling my body, eyes and ears, I plead desperately for an escape. I do not know who to ask, but if there is something out there, I need its help. I feel like I have never been so alone in my life.

When I was young, my mother – like many Punjabi mothers – would assuage my fears of all things by reminding me to repeat "Waheguru Satnam." I would awake from a nightmare and she would say, "It's okay. Just say *Waheguru Satnam.*" Repeating those words as a youngster gave me comfort, and today, the words rung in my ears as a soothing melody.

On the docks overlooking the river that afternoon, the words began to flow slowly from my lips in a low whisper. I am not sure why that mantra entered my consciousness. The phrase, recorded four centuries ago, seemed to be the gift and answer I longed for. I was not religious. I was raised as a regular Canadian kid of two hardworking Indian immigrants. I spent my afternoons playing hockey and discovering bugs. I attended Sunday school with some of the neighbourhood kids, only because they were going. I had no connection to my parents' faith or the bearded priests in turbans that sang hymns in an unfamiliar language at the local temples.

That day, those words entered my mind and changed my life in moments. Later, I was to find their meaning. The first word "Waheguru" derives from Persian and Sanskrit to mean "the wonderful divine that brings one from spiritual darkness to light." Satnam can be broken down to "Sat" meaning existence as well as truth and "Naam" meaning divine essence.

After some time, the words I spoke became rhythmic. Overwhelmed by the grandness of the mountain, the river and the sun, I began to understand my own insignificance. That moment humbled me. Here I stand, fully consumed by my anxiety, fears, hopes, sense of loathing, but I am insignificant! I am but a small part of a much larger, complex scheme. It is one thing to know that, but it is entirely another, to feel that. I found myself in a trance repeating

the mantra. All other thoughts disappeared from my mind. For the first time in my life, my mind became calm and relaxed. In this state of complete surrender, I kept repeating the words and with true humility, I reflect upon how insignificant and powerless I am and on the higher entity, the creator of all things.

This sudden foray into a neutral state of mind produced clarity. From this state of consciousness I entered a mind state that was beyond the description of my limited words. In that open air, cocooned by the mountains, breathing in the smell of the river, with sunshine streaming over my face, my body and mind felt illuminated. In an instant, I ceased to be. I was at once a part of the air around me, the soil beneath me, and the sights and smells surrounding me. My whole self disappeared into the energy around me. Peace. Sweetness. Bliss. Perfection. I needed nothing at that moment. I had everything. I felt fulfilled.

For the first time in my life, everything was as it was supposed to be. I had felt joy and happiness before, but no moment of joy, no moment of pure unadulterated laughter, had ever made me feel this way. My anxiety and fears vanished in an instant. My mind was filled with peace, calm and clarity. I wanted to dwell in that moment of perfection indefinitely. As suddenly as it had arrived, it left me just the same. I did not know what had just occurred but knew that I loved it and wanted more. After this experience, I realized that this was the last time that the loneliness and emptiness I grappled with for years would inflict me. Somehow I reached out when I felt alone and realized that I was not – nor would be – alone.

The impact of those few minutes spent on an empty dock, sent me on a decade long journey to find the peace I coveted my entire life. I searched through different religious and spiritual texts and found that spirituality begins where both the mind and heart meet. The journey led me to study neurology and quantum physics and inspirational poetry. I traveled to India twice. I eventually learned the truth of that experience.

There is a state of consciousness that human beings of any background can reach regardless of their religious beliefs. There are steps that I stumbled upon during that day, which are described in detail in eastern scriptures. In the quest for true fulfillment, one must identify the traps of the mind and calm it. Only after subduing the ego can one attempt to attain attachment to the one thing that is eternal. These things, when done together, can lead to true fulfillment. Bliss becomes attainable.

During a moment in the throes of deafening darkness and anguish, a plea for help was answered. "One in his mind will find gems, jewels and rubies if he were to act upon and listen to the true word." Guru Nanak Dev Ji (Japji Sahib).

A WOMAN POSSESSED
by Nancy Jonah

"SUCH STRANGENESS CANNOT BE explained. There are no rational words to explain how my life—how meeting Him so changed my life." With deep, dark eyes, Magda looked out at the crowd. There were so many people, all watching her with such amazement as though they could sense power or energy coming from her, but how could she explain it was not her energy they were sensing.

"Lord Jesus, please give me words to speak."

With an aching back and blistered feet, Joshua returned from the timber-haul to find Magda playing alone in the dirt. There were tracks of muddy hand prints smearing her orange dress, and her sandaled feet were ankle deep squishing through the sand. Digging to her elbows, she moulded the clay to form a river barge and castle wall. Behind the wall was a mound of dirt, probably supposed to be a castle.

Watching the little girl dig so intently, he regretted being so harsh with her. More than regret it, it could make no sense of it. Sweet little Magda. With her round cheeks and wide dark eyes that looked at him with such a lack of understanding. He was not an angry man

and could not reason why she should bring forth such rage in him. His confusion held him to the village gate and, feeling he could go no further, he slumped against the wall.

His daughter patted the sand smooth and looked up with searching eyes. Recognition hit him, and revulsion. In his daughter's upturned face, he did not see her mother's humble beauty, but a Roman's haughtiness. Her gaze stopped at a wild lily growing from the wall, and up she bounded. She plucked it with tenderness and with equal care centred it in the mud mound — flag in the castle.

The lily did not look straight or maybe it needed something to go with it. Magda leaped up, about to rush back to the wall to pick a red thistle that would go perfectly.

Everything stopped. After having been gone for so many days, her father was looming over her. Beneath his gaze she stood still, suddenly aware of how dirty she was. Dirt blackened her hands, nails, sandals, and toes. At least she could hide her hands in her dress, but wriggling her toes just squished the mud out — making them even worse. It seemed a long time, standing there looking at her dirt and waiting for her father to erupt. She did not dare look up.

His hand took hers, and she was sure he was going to scold her for the blackness of her hands and the dirt beneath her nails. Instead he linked his hand with hers.

"Magda." His hand was too big for hers, but he did not seem angry. Not sure she should, she slowly looked up. He did not look angry, just sad and very tired.

"Magda, you are such a pretty girl. You really ought to keep yourself tidy."

That was all he said and after that he did not seem so scary.

As soon as Magda was old enough to earn her own bread, she left the village. On a bright early morning, she filled a blanket with her clay pots and took them to market. Not sure where to go, she walked between the stalls looking for a friendly face, but the men who smiled looked more frightening than those who scowled. Her feet were getting tired and her pack heavy, when she turned a corner and saw a woman sitting in a trance. On a mat, she rocked back and forth and gazed into the flames of a fire pit. The woman began to speak, but with a voice unlike any Magda had ever heard. So frightening was the sound, she would have run away but for being too tired and having no place to run.

For all its drama, the trance ended simply enough. The

woman blinked, stretched her arms and legs, and looked at the man standing a few feet from her. He did not look happy. While the strange voice rose from the woman's throat, as though rising from a pit, he had been careful to keep back from her. Once the woman returned to herself, he rushed to her feet and they seemed to be arguing. Only for a moment, though; he dropped a coin in her hand, then turned and stomped away.

Magda went to stand before the woman.

"That was amazing! How did you do that? Could you show me?"

The woman blinked at her, looking ordinary and not how Magda expected a witch to look.

"What do you have there?" she asked Magda.

Magda showed her the clay pots.

This was how Magda came to share a stall with Dorcas, the market witch. While Magda spent her days turning rich earth into clay water jugs, bowls and heavy mugs, Dorcas told fortunes by throwing runes.

One day after weeks of their working together, Dorcas asked, "You're not going to see the desert prophet?" The desert prophet was a common topic among people passing through the market.

Magda shook her head not looking up from the clay her fingers were diligently working into a water pitcher.

"He is not calling himself a prophet." This was said by a woman who had stopped to look at a mug.

Annoyed, Magda's hand slipped.

"So what is he calling himself?" Dorcas asked.

"A voice of one calling in the desert."

"A voice! What is that supposed to mean?" Magda asked with irritation.

"I heard he eats locusts." A man came behind the woman, and she left with him without buying the mug.

"I'm glad you're not going," Dorcas said, "I have a bad feeling about him."

For all the prophet's calls for repentance, more and more people came to see Dorcas and Magda learned much from her.

On hearing of the desert prophet's arrest, Magda was glad. People would realize their foolishness and sense would be restored. No one would follow a jailed prophet.

Magda was wrong. Sense was not restored. Instead, his

followers just moved their obsession to Jesus of Nazareth. Such fools! Fury filled her just to look at them. How could they not see that God would not allow a true prophet to be jailed?

Each day her contempt for the people and hatred for the man deceiving them grew. All she could feel was rage. Dorcas was the first to know. Before there was even whispering, she raised her head from the runes and looked at Magda with a pale horrified seemingly pained face. Saying not a word and taking nothing, she got up and ran.

Whispers, pointing fingers, and a gleeful cry, "He is coming!" Everyone was so excited; whether believing him a prophet or a madman, all wanted to see him.

Fury and disgust exploded in Magda. These people so easily turned. Breathing hatred and rage in deep gulps, she got up and followed the mob to the prophet. There were so many people, many seeming to have come from great distances. How could she know which one was the prophet? But somehow she did. Her rage grew when she looked at him. Lead by her fury, she cut through the crowd until only a few feet from him. From her throat a cry rose, so scornful she did not recognize it as her own, ripping through her lips.

"What do you want with us, Jesus of Nazareth? Have you come to destroy us?" Frightened but not able to stop, the scornful mocking continued, "I know who you are—the Holy One of God!"

"Be quiet," He answered the voice and it quieted. Magda opened her mouth again, needing to explain but no words would come. How she wanted to run away, but she could not move, not even enough to turn from his gaze. Her eyes felt so wide and she could see nothing but Him and the light surrounding Him. Blinking did not help, and tears would not come.

"Come out of her," He said.

As though thrown to the ground by a violent cough, she landed at His feet, her anger gone.

MY NEIGHBOURHOOD
by Fatmatta R. Kanu

WE HAVE A SAYING in Sierra Leone: "A good neighbour is better than a relative who lives far away."

Freetown (the capital of Sierra Leone) is a dusty, sun-bathed city on Africa's west coast. The western part of the city is bordered by the Atlantic Ocean and has some of the most beautiful beaches in the region. In the background, an untidy mass of hills rises up against the skyline. In the mid 1400s, during the rainy season, Portuguese trader Pedro da Cintra, inspired by the growling thunder clap against the hills named the area Serra Lyoa (Lion Mountains).

Between then and the late 1950s and 1960s, when the wave of independence swept across most of West Africa, Sierra Leone went through different phases: trading with explorers, which developed into the slave trade, and then colonization. In 1961 Sierra Leone became independent from Britain.

In the early 1990s, Freetown had become the hub of politics, trade and culture in the small West African nation. On the political front, the country was ruled by a military junta, which had seized control from the elected government of Joseph Momoh in 1992. The Head of State was a 32-year old army captain named Valentine

Strasser.

In the city, when a new family arrived in the neighbourhood, its members went to the other homes in the surrounding area and introduced themselves. Reciprocal visits followed and within a short time, the newcomers got to know the people around them. They became a part of the whole neighbourhood.

I lived in a residential area in the western side of the city locally known as the Quarry. The houses were spaced about thirty to fifty feet apart, with trees and shrubbery separating the homes. We dropped in on one another to visit or ask for favours. We did not need to call ahead and inform them of your visit. We could, at any time during the day, go into a neighbour's house to chat and relax.

Like the adults, the children in the neighbourhood became friends. They took turns playing at each other's homes. Whichever house they chose to spend their day, the parents took care of all the children.

If there was a problem in any of the homes, it became a shared issue. For example, someone lost consciousness, and just one cry brought the neighbours rushing over to help. One person attended to the invalid, another called an ambulance, and others moved the invalid as required. This type of collective intervention was and still is the way of life in all of the neighbourhoods I lived in, in Sierra Leone.

One particular incident comes to mind. Adjacent to my house, on a large plot of land, grew about half a dozen fruit trees. The caretaker of the land and some of her family lived in a small house built of corrugated iron sheets on this land. It was July, the rainy season that Pedro de Cintra had famously experienced, now at the height of its power. On this night, the thunder roared with a terrible crackling anger, the rain sounded like a tumbling waterfall, and the lightning flashed through the sky dragging along the roaring thunder. The gusting wind lifted the roofs of houses and tossed them on the ground and on top of other houses. There was the cling clang of poles, dustpans and anything else in the path of the wind banging against the walls of houses.

Terrified, we sat inside our locked houses, when suddenly there was a huge bang that sounded like a bomb explosion, nearby. Then we heard people screaming. I moved towards the window and pulled back the curtains to look outside. Indeed something terrible had happened. One of the big mango trees in the adjacent plot of land had been uprooted by the wind, landing on the caretaker's

small house. A number of people were trapped inside! How could these people get help? The military rulers had imposed a 7 p.m. to 6 a.m. curfew at that time. The cries of trapped victims became louder.

No one wanted to venture outdoors for fear of being arrested by soldiers who patrolled the area to enforce the curfew! My heart thudding with fear, I looked through the sheets of rain, for any signs of movement within the house. I saw none.

To my relief, my neighbour, who lived opposite my house, Saio Kanu (no relation) pulled aside his blinds too. I timidly opened my window just enough for him to see me and shouted as loudly as I could, "A tree has fallen on the small house beside your house. I do not see anyone coming out."

"Yes, I know," he replied, "We have to do something." As we yelled to each other across the street, we came up with answers.

"The best thing to do at this moment, "he said, "is to call the Army Headquarters. I have the number. I will also call the two police divisions that serve this area. You call the military hospital. Do you have the number?"

"Yes I do, and I will also call a couple of doctors," I said. "We must get help in a hurry." I ran to the phone to make the calls. Mercifully, there were responses. Within a few minutes, Army Headquarters sent a van with soldiers. An ambulance and a police car also arrived. They knocked on my door and Mr. Kanu's door. We both joined them outside to give the information about the people inside the hut and what we saw and heard.

While we were talking to a couple of the officers, other members of the teams worked on getting those trapped inside, out of the hut. It took a number of men to pull down some of the tree branches. They had to cut open part of the window to slowly assist the occupants inch by inch, out of the house. Two elderly women, one young man and a little boy were rescued.

One young woman, Yealie, could not come out. She could not move, pinned down by the weight of one of the boughs of the tree. She could hear the questions we yelled in her direction. She managed to whisper that her chest and head were free but that the rest of her body was trapped. We ran to bring tools and implements – axes and machetes – that could be used to free her.

Parts of the tree trunk had to be carefully cut to lift some of the weight off the building. We made another opening close to the spot where the woman lay, to allow the officers to drag her out of

the damaged property. By the time they took her out, she had bled profusely and much weakened.

It was obvious that her injuries were serious. They took the young woman to the army hospital immediately, for treatment. The other four victims were taken into my sitting room. We treated their various injuries in the house, after which, they were taken to the hospital for observation.

The next day, the hospital discharged all of the people, except Yealie. The officers brought them back to Saio and me. They had no house to go to. The steady stream of people who came to the scene for days after the event could not believe that any one had escaped alive.

I offered to take the stranded people in until their relatives could find them a home. Yealie was released from hospital three days after the incident. Although she needed more time in a hospital, the bed was needed for new patients. She joined the others at my house. The army hospital continued to treat them as outpatients.

The other neighbours, including Saio and his wife, Yabome, helped provide for the needs of the five people. A neighbourhood donation drive was started. This brought in clothes, household utensils and school materials for the young boy. Saio and Yabome stored the items. When the neighbours left my house three weeks later, they had enough to start afresh in their new home.

These people, their families, friends, our other neighbours and even people from further away, thanked us, the two Kanu families, for making a timely intervention at a time when it was too dangerous to even open a window. Our daring actions that night helped save the lives of our neighbours.

However, we also had neighbours who had difficulties getting along with others. I had two such neighbours, a couple with whom I never exchanged a greeting for some two or more years and another neighbouring house whose occupants were anti-politician. They held the view that everything that went wrong in the country was to be blamed on politicians. My husband happened to be part of the government that had been ousted by the 1992 military coup.

Many people in the community believed that politicians got rich at the expense of the people they were supposed to serve. During our arguments, which became quite heated at times, I reminded them that blanket statements against any group of people were at best, misguided. I told them that my family, for example, had worked hard for many years to acquire everything we had. Both

my husband and I had succeeded in making names for ourselves before he entered politics. These kinds of neighbours were the exception to the friendly neighbourly attitude I generally enjoyed in my country.

I must say, however, I have learnt that in my absence, my "unfriendly" neighbours have intervened on my behalf when they see the people living in my house do anything they consider wrong around my compound, just like any other neighbour would do. Even though I am far away from Freetown, good neighbours are still helping to look after my property.

THE BRIDGE ON BLOOR
by Perparim Kapllani

THE SILHOUETTE, A LONELY ghost, lifts his arms up toward the sky and screams in a language unknown. Screams and listens to the echo. This short man is mysterious with a childish look, membrane skin covers his arms, but his eyeglasses betray him. His name is Desmodus Ruphus, a night bat. He stands in the middle of the biggest bridge of Bloor and cries aloud. The phantom approaches the silhouette rapidly, staring unflinching. The screams horrify the phantom, bringing to mind someone who has fingers driven into his chest and tearing open his heart. The phantom shivers.

"This man can do something very dangerous," the phantom thinks as he runs, almost breathless.

"Hey! How can I help you, my friend?"

The silhouette turns his face toward the phantom but remains speechless wondering how a phantom could show up all of a sudden.

"Why did you scream, sir?" the phantom asks slowly and clearly.

The words resound into space. To the silhouette, this seeming giant human mocked him dragging his words. He puts his finger on

his lips and asks, "Do you hear the echo? The Dolphin Institute in Hawaii built a database of the kind of proteins a dolphin consumes, the quantity of fish, number of breaths per minute, the strange behaviour and wounds. They also have a database that determines the water conditions, the levels of microbes in water, the content of bacteria. The echolocation is a method of sense perception which some animals use for self orientation, to locate the obstacles, communicate with other animals, and find food. I use the echolocation method to orient myself on very dark nights; that's why I scream with my all strength."

"Where are you from, sir?"

"Bania Luka, Bosnia. I left my homeland when I was twelve years old, on a freight train to Croatia, after a group of Serbians killed my father, my grandmother, my grandfather, two aunts, and my uncle. They burned my house and abducted my cow. I left Croatia when I was twenty-one and stayed for seven months in Italy, after which I went to Canada. I have never seen my country after that and have no desire to ever go back there again."

He pauses and then sighs.

"I couldn't sleep last night. I saw my mother in my dreams, crying. I see the same dream over and over again, the same dream recurring for years. I see my Serbian neighbours come to my house when I was nine. I see a wild man undress my mother by force. I am shocked and totally weakened. He rapes my mother in front of my eyes. I see that shameful scene with me shaking and shivering with anger and fear. I don't recall how many minutes I stayed bewildered watching my mother moan and groan under that man. Those minutes seemed like hours. I come out of the house, go into the backyard, pull a stick off the fence and I return in once again. I attack the man with the stick till he gets off my mother, whose ears he was now slapping. He had slapped her so much that she became deaf for the rest of her life. She died two years ago. That terrible act changed me as a human, forever.

I kept my head down all my life, ashamed. When I am emotional, I come here and scream as much as I can till I feel free. Till I don't feel the emotional ball growing larger in my throat. Now, you, my dear phantom, you understand why I scream in the darkness on the biggest bridge of Bloor. I am a night bat after her death. I emit the screams, these terrible sounds which travel into space. I cannot orient myself however, I've lost the sense of echolocation."

"Will you return some day to Bania Luka?" the phantom asks.

"I can't go back. I am scared I may kill everyone who comes in

front of me, or I might get killed! The only thing I can do is to come here sometimes and start screaming. I scream out loud to free my pain."

The phantom is embarrassed. He slaps the silhouette affectionately. The tearful silhouette tries to stop sobbing. He invites the phantom to scream with him into the mysterious night. He puts his hands around his mouth and starts screaming. The phantom screams, too. Their screams are so loud, such as the stars can hear in the sky. The phantom screams louder than the silhouette. Then the silhouette screams louder than the phantom. They are a couple of wolves, very wild, who pour their hearts out onto the earth, without abandon. One can see the light in their eyes. The phantom screams over and over again, crazed with the magic of this evening. He looks down the bridge into the silent waters. He sees the sweet eyes of the silhouette's mother smiling from the waves of the Humber River.

BYE-BYE LOVE
by Sharon Knauer

DAVID WATCHED THE JANITOR swagger into the tiny laundromat bathroom, Comet in hand, toilet brush bristling from a thick leather tool belt. A super roll of paper towels was holstered in a plastic clip, officious keys clanked, J-cloths clustered in a damp droop on one hip, a feather duster puffed off the other. The sagging ass of his green work pants completed the ensemble. Power suit.

That's just fucking sad, David thought, and then clamped his mind down tight—for a nanosecond. And who's sad, huh? Who's the fucking sad man here? Who just spent two hours scrubbing every floor in a five-hundred-square-foot apartment and then stomped out the door to the Laundromat in regal, righteous wrath?

He jerked clothes out of the basket. If one pair of socks is an inside out ball of mold, I'm gonna kick your ass. I'm gonna tear your head off. I'm gonna . . .

You're gonna what?

He sagged against the Formica counter and let the hurt fester a bit.

Whites on the left. Colours on the right. Ben's yellow T-shirt, the one he'd bought for him in Trinidad two winters ago. It had

a florid, almost obscene, sunset stencilled on the front—the scarlet sun sinking into water so blue it didn't look real. Eye-catching camp. Ben wore it all the time, even to bed, but the stencil had faded now. The seams were a little fuzzy. The yellow had degenerated into a scummy cream and the sun was a sallow pink. The blue didn't even register.

He stuffed the T-shirt into an empty washing machine and followed it with a healthy dose of bleach. Bye-bye Caribbean beach at sunset. Bye-bye love.

Ben's jeans went in with the T-shirt, and his black work socks, now turned right side out, assorted dress shirts, underwear that David could barely manage to touch, and finally, the chinos. He slammed the lid down and shoved quarters into the slots, rammed the metal tongue into the change collector and watched the light turn green on the washer panel. Wash cycle. You bet.

Why Ben? After five years of laughing together over a glass of wine and seared tuna at dinner when David's hospital shift coincided with Ben's office hours, after five years of sharing a bed and bodies, after five years of making a life.

Ben said he had gotten drunk last night. David didn't know if that was true or not, he'd been at work from seven to seven—starting IV's, taking blood pressure and soothing troubled brows. And Ben? He'd soothed more than a troubled brow. He'd wagged his ass at one of those sculpted, perfect bodies in Wet Lips and instead of laughing it off, instead of coming home and teasing David with it, instead of making it into a kind of foreplay . . . instead of that . . .

Ben had come home and puked. The evidence had still been there this morning, glazing the bathroom floor in chunky, shining mucous. Until David scrubbed it, then scoured the hallway, the living room, the kitchen and the tiny front entrance. From there he'd moved to the laundry basket.

Of course, the puke *could* have just been a slightly distasteful indiscretion, something to be dealt with and not discussed. He'd seen enough puke in his life and at work to know how unimportant it was. But Ben had confessed at the breakfast table, his face a blaze of shame and uncertainty. And all David had heard was the undertone, an unmistakeable background of thrill and triumph. The forty-year-old Ben still had what it takes.

The bastard had liked it. He'd more than liked it. He'd loved it.

More bleach.

David emptied his pockets. Did he have enough quarters to run Ben's clothes through the washer a second time? He did. Just enough. Two washes, half a gallon of bleach. Forty minutes in the dryer. A careful folding. He'd have two dimes, three nickels and two pennies left. Thirty-seven cents.

Not enough for a beer. He'd have to go home and get his wallet for that. Maybe he'd hit Wet Lips. Been years since he'd picked up Ben there. Been years since he'd picked up anything but laundry and dirty dishes.

David lifted the washer lid to watch the yellow T-shirt slog against the rest of Ben's clothes. Sunset bled into the white shirts, denim leaked into khaki, something that might have been Ben's underwear—a bleach-pocked surge of cloth—swam its way to the surface and was sucked underneath by a school of greyish socks.

The toilet flushed in the Laundromat bathroom. The cleaner strutted out, triumphant arsenal holstered back on his belt. Bleach and Comet scented the air. He nodded at David. David nodded back.

An excerpt from the historical novel
FLOWER POWER
by Bianca Lakoseljac

"Flower Power" is a historical novel set in present day Toronto, with a backdrop of the 1967 Art Symposium in High Park — as part of Canada's Centennial celebrations. The novel follows two mother/daughter stories. One is set in 1967 with Liza, and the second in 2009, with Liza's daughter, Blossom, as the protagonist. The novel draws on the events of 1967 and the anti-Vietnam war movement, symbolized by some of the art work created during the Art Symposium, such as Mark di Suvero's sculpture Flower Power, after which, the novel takes its title.

Toronto: April 20, 1967

THERE WAS NO MISTAKING the whirring of the helicopter. Liza could feel anticipation mount in the large gathering on Nathan Philips Square. All eyes rose to the swishing blades nearing the three concrete arches that spanned the reflecting pool.

The aircraft hovered for a few minutes, and then rose up in a wide circle over the Square.

"They must be marvelling at the vista from above!" Anna exclaimed over the helicopter noise. "Admiring the new city hall."

"We should take a ride sometimes. I'd love to see the half pipes from a helicopter," Liza called out.

She knew a helicopter ride is possible any time, but with Anna it would be more interesting. Anna knew the local history and issues—an interest she'd picked up from her parents who had been members of the local historical board—as if she were an old-timer and not just twenty six. She had joined the Department of Culture straight after high school. Now, the youngest office manager, energetic, perfect 5'4", dark hair spilling down her back, and never a dab of makeup, Anna became the 'voice of experience' for the new staff.

Ever since the twenty three year old Liza began working in the same office, Anna had taken the younger co-worker under her wing. And Liza, a recent University of Toronto graduate who loved high heels fancy dresses, and who wouldn't be caught dead without full makeup, wondered if she'd ever come close to Anna's poise.

Liza had been planning to get an aerial view of Vijo Revell's modern architecture since Toronto's new city hall opened in 1965. The design, one of over 500 submitted through an international competition under the terms set out by the International Union of Architects, was chosen by a panel of judges. Two years later, the complex of structures representing two eyelids and a pupil was still the 'buzz of the town' as well as a source of controversy.

Anna placed her hand above her eyes to shade it from the sun and peered at the building. "Eyelids, ha? Seeing it from above *is* a way to tell."

Liza nodded. "I'd like to see if that round council hall in the middle makes me think of a pupil."

"That flying saucer in the middle's supposed to be a pupil? Of an eye?" a woman standing next to Liza interjected. "I can't help but overhear the two of you. I read about that, somewhere. It's darn elegant, the whole design of it. But a pupil?"

"I think it looks like a UFO," a man nearby chuckled.

"No, no, it's a giant burger," another man mumbled, stuffing the last bite of burger in his mouth and wiping his hands on the legs of his jeans.

"Too modern for our city, too abstract," a woman in perfect coiffure dressed in a brown tweed suit, declared. She pointed to the red sandstone facade of the old city hall that blunted Bay Street at

Queen and added, "Totally out of character."

"We can't compare the new building to the old Romanesque city hall," Liza said, "The new design *is* modern, abstract, and different. As it should be."

"I love the new architecture," Anna scoffed looking at the man with a burger, "But the old city hall has its place too. Suddenly everyone sees it as an eyesore. People calling for demolition."

"This is a historic moment," Liza said to Anna, "the chopper announcing the beginning of the big sculpt-in."

"Twelve sculptors from different parts of the world will invade High Park," a gravelly voice interjected. Both women turned. It was the man with the burger. He smiled playfully and winked. "The art will be ultra modern—no compromises here."

"It will shake up Toronto's art community in a big way," Liza said.

The man nodded good-humouredly and moved a step closer.

Liza flipped her hair and flashed him an enigmatic smile. "In fact, it'll shake up the image of Toronto."

The man moved another step closer. "Wouldn't that be grand? Shaking up this sleepy old town."

Anna gave him a look of annoyance.

"It all seems so symbolic, the contrast between the old and the new," Liza recapped, "the need for change."

Anna turned her back to the stranger. She linked her arm under Liza's and they moved several steps away.

The white helicopter hovered a few minutes longer, and then descended on the large concrete slabs in front of city hall. The smiling face pressed into the side window and a Mayor William Dennison sitting beside, waved. He stepped out, stooped over, and ran to the side, beaming at the crowd.

Two other men emerged. One was Ontario Education Minister Bill Davis, followed by a tall, lanky man.

Liza nudged Anna, "That has to be Len Lye."

Anna slipped her glasses on for a closer look. "That American known for those strange metal sculptures? I thought he was much older."

"He's 66. Born in 1901."

"Somebody's done her research."

"His photo is true to his physique," Liza continued. "Hooked nose, rectangular glasses propped up on top of his head." She paused

and looked at him for a moment. "He reminds me of a large crane, the bird as well as the machine."

Anna laughed. "His appearance does fit his reputation."

"Of an eccentric genius?" Liza raised herself on tiptoes and peered through the crowd. "And look at his beard! It *is* shaped to resemble the double helix."

"I read about that somewhere. Apparently the discovery of the DNA spiral had a great impact on him. And his beard."

The two women smiled at each other and Liza added, "He has been interested in scientific discoveries. Loves scientific journals. He used the helix as inspiration for some of his sculptures. Apparently, he believes that we can still learn much by exploring this form."

"That all sounds impressive," Anna smirked. "But does anyone know whether the beard came before or after the DNA discovery?"

"Not sure," Liza laughed. "Though he's the reason I'd be here even if it wasn't part of my job."

"I didn't know you're such a fan."

"He'll be demonstrating the principle of kinetic art. Showing a film of his work. The title is *Free Radicals*."

"Did you ask to be put on the symposium committee?"

Liza shrugged. "I was assigned. And thrilled to be part of all this."

"What else do you know about Len Lye? Does he like his coffee black? Does he sleep naked?"

Liza laughed. "He believed that motion could be an element of the language of art. Now, that's innovative."

Anna glanced at her watch. "This job does have its benefits. Meeting all these artists. Too bad I have to run."

"Aren't you staying for the ceremonies?" Liza asked. "Irving Burman and I are taking Len Lye and Armand Vaillancourt on a tour of the city. I was hoping you'd join us."

"The handsome Montréaler? Sorry kiddo. I've got to get back to the office. Late staff meeting. Besides, you've got to get your feet wet sooner or later. You'll be great."

"But I'm counting on you."

Anna skimmed the crowd as if searching for someone. "Got to run. You'll have to fill me in tomorrow." Rushing off, she turned and chuckled, "And stay away from strange men."

Liza felt a twinge of panic. She'd met Burman briefly once before. Will he even remember her?

From where she stood, Burman looked middle-aged and conservative. He began to speak to the gathering, expressing great interest in working in High Park, in his own city. Liza gathered that he was easygoing and approachable, and she breathed a sigh of relief.

Gerald Gladstone, another Toronto sculptor and the mastermind behind the project greeted the men. He scanned the crowd and spotting Liza, waved her over. He introduced her to Armand Vaillancourt who shook her hand enthusiastically. Vaillancourt's long hair and beard made him appear much younger than thirty five. He seemed closer to her own age, and Liza felt her apprehension melting.

Gladstone pulled out a stack of photos and sketches from his briefcase. "We forgot to post some of the artists' info," he said to Liza. "I need a few moments with the mayor before his speech."

"I'll post them on the board," Liza said, taking the material from his hands headed towards the display.

She was done just as Mayor Dennison began with the announcements. He emphasized the significance of the sculpture symposium and its role in the Canada-wide centennial celebrations. He was confident the sculpt-in would bring international attention to Canada's artistic heritage.

Bill Davis took over the lectern. He informed the audience that Gordon Awde, the symposium co-coordinator, was successful in assembling supplies. Much was donated by local businesses and the community and some of the equipment had been lent to the artists.

Each speaker was awarded a thunderous applause. At last, the part Liza had been waiting for most of the day began—Len Lye's short black and white film, *Free Radicals.* As the white pattern zigzagged on the screen to the soundtrack of African drum music, Liza felt transfixed into another place and time.

Lye announced that his High Park creation would be a metal pole eight stories high with a large ball at the top. The audience was ecstatic.

"This is better than I ever imagined!" Liza exclaimed.

"You always talk to yourself, young lady?" a gravelly voice behind her asked.

Liza glanced sideways, one way and the other. No one made eye contact. Her attention focused back on the crowd. She felt the excitement in the air, carried on a tempestuous breeze that quickly swept through Nathan Philips Square.

Wake up from your sleep, Toronto! The hypnotic beating of the drums is heralding a new era, her thoughts raced.

Gladstone approached. "The tour of the city was called off," he announced. "The artists have other plans. Thanks Liza. We'll keep it in mind for another time."

Liza sat at the edge of the reflecting pool. She didn't feel like going home, not just yet. Before her she could see the concrete bottom of the shallow pool. When she looked a bit farther toward city hall, the arches dipped into the water as if it were bottomless. The sky and the clouds mingled with the gentle ripples unfurled by the wind.

Among the ripples, a reflection of a male figure formed, only a few feet from her own, then joined with her own — the two effigies wobbling among the white clouds and patches of blue.

She turned. *Him again?* Instead of a burger, he was eating a sugar dusted donut out of a paper bag.

"Oh, this?" he said, pointing to the donut, as if they'd had an ongoing conversation. He crumpled up the bag noisily, turned on his heels, and holding the paper ball behind his back, threw it over his head and into the garbage container as if it were a basketball hoop. To her surprise, it hit its target.

He extended his hand to her.

"David."

"Just... David?"

"That's it. David."

"O K. Liza."

"Just Liza?"

"Yep."

He smiled and nodded. His round-framed sunglasses drooped down on his nose. Low on his forehead, flame red curls bobbed as if they were a wig.

FLESH
by Karen Lam

You can't trust him because he doesn't trust himself.

HE REMOVES A FRUIT from the wooden bowl; despite the abundance of apples and bananas, he chooses a lonely orange. I don't know why he smiles, for an orange is a sexless fruit – at least apples are associated with sin, and bananas are structurally phallic – an orange is uninterestingly androgynous.

I watch his silhouette under the veil of darkness. With the moonlight streaming through the tiny apartment window, I find myself imagining the poetic curvature of his spine. I'm not cold, but I shiver a little, not knowing his purpose and fearing the consequence.

I wonder what he's doing in my apartment at this hour. I almost wish I could pay him to leave so I wouldn't feel like the *other* woman. Somehow annotating the evening with an orange means only trouble will ensue.

I've been watching him, but I don't know if he has been watching me. We are worlds apart, but somehow geography and physics have now become only inches and centimetres.

He scares me. I'm scared of him.

He begins to peel the orange on the small of my back, stroking the delicate curves of citrus and watching single droplets of juice trickle — sticky and unforgiving. It feels strangely familiar, with his legs straddling on either side. His breath smells of whisky.

He begins at the base and pries at the rind with his fingernails. Pale half-moons against dimpled skin — a violated white. If he tears too quickly, or too violently, the orange will resist. There is care in his preparation. He wants to remove the peel in the least destructive way possible. Flesh waits, nubile and ready for consumption. I close my eyes as another drop of citrus falls onto my back. I sense his lips trembling, but it's his fingers I am aware of, quivering each time he applies pressure.

It is my first time.

I am not his first.

I glance at the orange peel and I am afraid to interrupt him. "May I turn around now?" I ask slowly and gently.

He places his hand over the spot where the orange had rested. Even though I can't see his face, I know he's looking at me as though I have forced him into committing an unforgivable act. "I'm..."

I speak into the pillow, damp with sleep and forgotten fairytales. The slight movement of my head makes him panic – he places his hands over my eyes before I can turn to face him.

"Please, don't look at me," he grunts. He pulls back his hands hurriedly after realizing they're sticky. "Sorry," he mumbles, fumbling with the elastic of his underwear.

"It's okay," I murmur, catching the look in his eyes as I decide to disobey him and turn around. I'm unsure of what he's trying to tell me. There's something in his eyes that I had neglected to notice before.

I barely know him.

I look again at the abandoned orange peel and realize now that we can never go back.

An excerpt from the novel
THE DRUMS CRIED
by John Maar

South Pacific, 1942

ON THE GRASS MAT spread out on the earthen floor of the frontless lean-to hut, the girl lay flat on her back, looking at her without moving an eyelid. Annie smiled at the poor soul. She had to be helped, but how could she do anything as awesome as delivering a dead baby from a thirteen-year-old with the means that she had? She looked at the girl. A couple of buds on her chest rippled with prominent ribs disproportionately small in comparison to the bulge of her belly. A bag full of bones described her perfectly.

Annie took a deep long breath. She had encountered many different emergencies at the colony, but this one was something totally different. A trauma of this nature required the attention of a gynaecologist and a well-equipped hospital. Annie stole a glance at the villagers squatting in dozens on the hillside in front of the entrance of the lean-to, hoping to catch a tiny hint from anyone of what she should do. What she saw was not encouraging. They just gazed at her in silence. Not one of the men had adorned himself to indicate a sign of a higher rank. They had left the medical crisis for

her to resolve. She had to be it all — the witch doctor, the surgeon and her own nursing assistant.

"Mary," she said to the older sister "Tell your people that I need some water. They should also build this fire."

The big woman seemed to have shrunk in size. "Oh nurse Annie," she spoke in Pidgin English, the universal language, used on these South Pacific islands. "Water him far away. Wood too, him no got. Night time, him too dark. No can see."

"Oh, for heaven' sake! You made me climb this mountain to help your sister get well and now I don't want to hear any of your NO CAN words! I need warm water and I want it now."

The girl, flat on her back on the floor, puckered her lips, her eyes enlarged stared up at the smoke-stained ceiling of the thatched hut. Annie kneeled beside her, placed a gentle hand on her naked shoulder. The girl's eyes filled up with tears.

"What's your name?"

Annie expected to hear a long, foreign sounding word, but the girl said feebly, "Mary."

Annie grinned, "I guess I'll have to call you Mary II. Your sister and I met first, so she better stay Mary I. She then placed a soothing hand on the girl's forehead, "What I'm going to do will hurt, but I promise I'm going to make you get well."

I certainly will try, she thought to herself, aware of her pulse thumping in her ears.

"Mary, I need that water!"

Mary translated, after which a bunch of villagers made torches from sticks of wood and hurried off downhill to fetch firewood and water. They brought in a rather large cauldron of heavy cast iron from under one of the huts, and hung it above the fire burning right at the entrance of the open lean-to.

Annie had to help the girl deliver that baby. She had to do it somehow. A caesarean cut seemed the most likely answer, but the very thought of it gave her the shivers. To do a major surgery on a girl like this one without anaesthetics was simply terrifying. What if the girl bleeds to death? Her life seemed to be already hanging on a thread. And then it came to her. Annie looked down at her hands. They were quite small. Thank YOU. You up there, for enlightening me, she thought.

"Mary, find me a couple of strong armed women, please? We need them to hold down your sister."

Moments later, with her face sweaty and flushed, Mary I

ushered into the hut a pair of young women sporting large auras of hair on their heads, with grass skirts , bare breasted with seashell necklaces adorning their shapely necks, and the ever-present tattoos marking their pretty faces and feminine arms.

"Him two-fella you been ask," Mary said. "But me... me like go away. Me afraid look-look see you cut-cut him open belly belong sister belong me."

"Oh, no!" Annie could feel a surge of power fill her chest. "I need everyone here to give me a hand. Stay and translate for me. Tell them that I want them to keep your sister's life from getting away. The pulse that they can feel in her wrists is her life. Tell them not to let her life go." The two women took the young patient by the wrists as instructed.

More villagers kept arriving on the opposite bank of the hill like silent shadows. They squatted down to see what was most likely the performance of their life. Brushing a strand of hair from her forehead, Annie realized that she should put up a curtain of grass mats to give this young mother dignity, but there was no time for niceties. She threw a towel across the girl's torso. Kneeling down in a discreetly executed curtsy, she placed the scalpel back into the bucket. The remains of the unfortunate pregnancy would have to be extracted by hand.

"Mary," she said to the older sister in a voice dry and strange to herself, "can I have a rope of some sort?"

Mary hobbled over to a neighbouring hut and hurried back with a crudely braided length of jungle creepers in hand. Annie tied up the four corners of the floor mat, and then wrapped a pair of towels around the young girl's knees and a large one behind her back. The patient was then raised gently a couple of feet off the ground, under the beam spanning the entrance of the hut.

Drums came alive with a flurry of nerve wracking, "Clog-clog, clogum, boop-boop brom-broom's!"

Taking a bottle of methylated spirit from the bucket, Annie asked the older sister to bring her a couple of coconuts. "Your sister has to be given some sort of anaesthetic."

Mary I used a machete to chop off the tops of two bulging green coconuts. Annie took a long soothing drink of sweet, cool water from one, and then spilt out some of it from the second coconut, topping it with alcohol, Pakua style. Raising the head of the patient, she brought it to her lips. "Drink this," Annie said softly. "It'll make you fall into a deep sleep. When you wake up, you're

will be a completely new girl."

Scooped inside the mat, with her knees strapped high and wide, Mary II slurped the water from the coconut till empty, closed her eyes, after which she became deathly still. Annie felt her wrist, and finding a strong pulse, sent her silent thanks in her mind to who ever was listening.

The villagers didn't understand what was going on and they began speaking to each other in agitated tones "Tell them not to worry," she said to Mary I. "Your sister is asleep. I hope she will not feel the pain as I bring out the baby. But, while I do so, tell them not to allow her life to get away in their minds. Tell them that we all want Mary II to wake up in the morning alive and well."

Mary spoke to the crowd gesticulating with her hands, after which they settled down, their eyes riveted into the fire lit hut.

"Please Lord give me the strength," Annie sent her prayer upwards. "I'm not asking anything for myself. It's for this girl. The poor thing's worse off than a leper. Let her come out of this alive and well."

Kneeling down onto the earthen floor, she smeared her right hand thickly with greasy ointment from a no-label can and then proceeded to do something under the cover of the towel, something which she had never expected to do, ever. The procedure took long and the patient resisted the women with surprising strength. Annie felt awkward and ineffective, and she took stops when the girl objected a bit more vigorously

The night breeze kept blowing smoke into the hut till finally she could hardly see, breathe, or think. Just as well, though! Annie eventually decided. The smoke distracted her mind from the emotional aspect of this procedure.

This was indeed, the closest anyone could ever be physically to another human being. She held the tiny dead body inside a live one — here in this smoke-filled hut, her closest encounter to life and death! Tears flowed from her eyes, blinded by the smoke, yet the presence of a higher feeling of what had happened seemed real and powerful. Annie wiped her tears with her left forearm and then commenced extracting the baby with a number of rather assertive tugs.

Mary II screamed in pain and a couple of strong armed men rushed over to help restrain her. Then, she mercifully lapsed into unconsciousness. Once again as Annie began to work with her hands, they all seemed like they had ceased to breathe, not wanting

to miss a thing. Annie extracted the baby, glad that it had come out in one piece. She also brought out the afterbirth, placing it all on a banana leaf spread on the floor. When she indicated with her eyes that she was done with the procedure, a burst of speedy soft drumming and handclapping erupted from the audience.

Annie concentrated on cleaning the young not-to-be mother with warm water, and then with the help of the women, lowered her gently onto a clean mat of grass spread out flat on the floor. She covered the girl from neck to her knees with a new towel, indicating that the show had ended. The villagers stood up on stiff legs, commenting on things they had seen, while their eyes centered on the foreign woman in awe. As they headed towards their huts for the night, their excited voices mingled with the howls and cries from the night creatures of the jungle.

The older sister had disappeared unseen into the darkness without saying a word. Annie grinned to herself. Mary I was probably lured away by one of the healthy young men.

Alone with the patient, Annie drank the contents of a whole coconut and then, unable to stand on her feet any more, eased her shoulder onto the hard packed ground and curled into the foetal position with the side of her face resting on the corner of the grass mat that the patient lay on.

"Thank you Lord for giving me the strength to…" she started praying. "Oh my gosh!" She gasped, propping herself back on her elbow. "Today is Christmas!"

She had been yanked out of bed by Mary I midday today and been so preoccupied that she had completely forgotten that it was Christmas. She let herself slip back on the ground and with her eyes heavy, she conked out before her head hit the mat.

"BOOOOOM! BOOOOM! BOOOM! Boom! Boom! Boom! Boom! Bom! Boom! Bom! Bom! Bom!" Someone drummed on the hollow log in the middle of the village. The beat tumbled and rolled like a heavy boulder, slowly at first, and then as it sped up, the thud- thud echoed far away through the tropical night to other native communities on similar mountain crests, telling them about the extraordinary deed that had taken place in this old hut.

THE GIRL IN THE WOODS
by Gemma Meharchand

NINA SAT AT A tiny table in Starbucks at the Eaton Centre, sipping a cup of chai.

Through the window she watched the clouds and blue sky reflect on the cool white, painted glass of the shopping centre and the surrounding office buildings, so like a Magritte painting she had once seen in the Art Gallery at Montreal, not long after she had arrived in Canada from her native African seaside town. She watched the old building next door, a frosted mocha cake as in a child's fairytale fantasy, the street filled with sunshine, and the shopping mall with scrubbed kids looking for adventure and clothes. An apple-cheeked pair of fashion statements sitting near the window smiled at her.

A van pulled up outside the mocha-frosted cake and delivered someone to the courthouse. She saw Kyle come in to the coffee shop and look around for her. He was the kind of guy the women gazed at with admiration. The kind she knew made them weak at the knees. They had a few moments together before she left for home.

She sprayed on *Chance* by Chanel as she left the Eaton Centre. She took the streetcar to the day camp. She and Eva would go home and watch TV.

As she drew near, she saw clusters of people and a few police cars. Something was not quite right. What could they be doing there? Only when she got to the camp she realized that Eva was not there. Eva had gone missing months before and the police had now given up the search. The police talked to people who may have seen something, but she had given up hope. She began to cry as the horrible thoughts flooded back on her, making her knees knock and her heart beat slower as she sat on the bench. She watched the children play in the fenced area where her daughter had been. She had left her country and come to Canada to improve her circumstances, only now, her child had disappeared.

Kyle, down on his knees, looked for the bracelet Nina had dropped. He cared little for the bruised knees from the little stones in the gravel yard at the corner. He groped around to find the eight thousand dollar bracelet that Nina had so carelessly thrown into the bushes, when teasing, he suggested it could be a fake. He had not expected this. She tore the elegant circle of silver and gems from her wrist and threw it over the fence into the patch of greenery that grew along one side of the vacant lot. Almost at once, he opened the gate and searched for the most expensive present he had ever given her, causing a startled flight of birds on the other side.

Nina stood with a mocking smile as he trod carefully through the bushes looking for the bracelet. He paused for a moment to say to her, "What in God's name were you thinking of, throwing that away?"

Nina saw his puzzled anger and realized that the charm was expensive. She joined him in the search. A few minutes later they found the bracelet and something else that surprised them. A backpack, tucked away in the lush growth, just like the one Eva had carried on the day she went missing. A Hello Kitty backpack bought by Kyle on a trip to the Cindy Store in the Eaton Centre. Eva had pointed it out to him and he had bought it for her.

Here was proof of her existence, a year after the search with the dogs and neighbours scouring parks and ravines. Kyle felt the dampness and chill in the air as he reached for the bag and picked it up. His hands trembled as he handed it carefully to Nina, who on her haunches reached out like a pale ghost as she whispered the name of her child.

"Eva... she must have been here since that day..."

Kyle had launched a separate search for Nina's daughter. This was the first real piece of evidence that seemed inches closer to finding Eva or what had happened to her. As Kyle crept closer to the spot where the backpack had lain, he caught a glint of the lost bracelet. He picked it up and placed it on Nina's arm. Then he walked to the car got his camera out, as Nina made the call to Sergeant McDowell who had been in charge of the case.

Eva looked at her friend who she camped with all summer and through the year. No insults from teachers, no bullies who hated her dark brown hairy looks, no more.

She spent her time looking for mushrooms to kill them all. She would learn the secrets of the wild, the mysteries of werewolves and trolls, from her friend who liked her body. Every day she had waited for her father outside a bar to take him home to dinner. Now she would end all this dark coldness.

An excerpt from the non-fictional story
SILOLE
by Braz Menezes

"Silole" is a story of a young man and a young woman born in Kenya; each of very different family and racial backgrounds, brought together by fate. It is set against the backdrop of British Kenya in mid 20th century, a society ruthlessly segregated by race, colour and ethnicity, and further defined by title and tribe, class, caste and creed... "We grew up all neatly labelled and classified as were the reptiles and rodents in Dr Leakey's nearby Coryndon Memorial Museum."

(1948)

SILOLE LAY IN THE dark, listening to the rain beating on the corrugated-iron roof. The rhythmic sound of the water formed a soft wrap around her and kept the *nyangaus*, monsters, at bay; just three years ago, when she was four, they loomed around in the dark, somewhere out there, and were so scary that one dared not even imagine what they looked like.

Now that she lived in Nakuru, her monsters still lurked

around, but this time manifested in a myriad of insecurities, which Aunty Mina's strict disciplinarian and authoritarian ways had ensured a deep embedding into her psyche. Somehow, she always managed to get herself into trouble, even when she tried her hardest not to, but she more than made up for it in mental agility and her sporting abilities, and was regarded as the tomboy in the family. Perhaps if her real mother was there, things might have been different.

She moved her body into a new position. Normally she and her stepsister, Doris, who shared a room, slept only in their knickers during the hot season, but now with the colder weather she wore the freshly washed and ironed flannel nightdress a European lady had given Aunty Mina at a St. Vincent de Paul Fund-Raising Bazaar just two weeks earlier. For added warmth, she tucked the grey Nakuru Brand army blanket around herself.

As she lay there, Silole tried to decipher what the rain was saying. Sometimes the rhythm formed itself into a tune, but she never stayed awake long enough to hear it. Today, just as she drifted off, the sound of a car drawing up next door registered somewhere in her mind, its wheels splashing through pools of rainwater. She thought she heard the sound of voices, Indian voices—somebody saying goodbye.

Light from the car's headlights shone through the flimsy curtain, illuminating the room. Careful not to wake Doris, Silole sat up and leaned across the bed to look out through the dirty windowpane. She wondered whether the car had come for the young Indian boy who had arrived next door earlier in the day while she had been playing with her doll in the garden. He had come right up to the hole in the kai-apple fence and looked at her through the gap.

"Hello, what's your name?" he had called out boldly. "I'm Orlando from Nairobi, but you can call me Lando. Everyone does."

Silole was at first unsure how to respond. She had never spoken to an Indian boy before. He was a little older than she was, slightly built, with a mop of straight black hair, sharp features, and strong good looks. He gave another "hello," this time with such a disarming grin that any misgivings she may have had quickly dissolved. Her curiosity got the better of her; she relaxed and walked up to the fence.

"My name is Silole, but my sisters call me Miri," she replied, "and this is Sudi. Say hello to Lando, Sudi." She straightened the

doll's pink limbs and held her upright, so the bright blue eyes opened wide and looked straight at him.

But Lando didn't look at the doll. He looked at Silole's head instead.

"Your hair is funny," he said. "It looks African, but it is orange. Did you paint it?"

Silole instinctively put her hand to her hair, as if to reassure herself it was still there, unchanged.

"I am not African," she said sharply. Even at seven she was aware that being coloured was bad, and being black was worse. "I am Shelishely. I'm from the Seychelles. Do you know where that is? My Aunty Mina and Uncle Dada are also Shelishely."

"I know where Seychelles is," Lando said. "It's where ships from Goa stop on the way to Mombasa. I know that because my Daddy came that way. He says there are pirates in the Seychelles. Do you know any pirates?"

"No," she replied. "But maybe my uncle knows some."

"Are you Catholic?" he asked, pointing to a small pendant hanging from a string around her neck.

"Dada told me I had to become Catholic, or the nuns wouldn't take me into their school," Silole said. "It's near Nairobi. Do you know my school?"

Lando didn't answer. "What's that?" he asked instead, pointing to a spot on her body just below her right shoulder.

"Nothing." She pulled her dress over to cover the scar.

"Wait!" he said, as she turned to go. "Look!" He pulled two bullet tips from his pocket and held them out to her.

"Where did you get them?"

"I can't tell you. Would you like one?"

She hesitated. "No. I'll get into trouble." Again she turned away.

"Can I have that stick?" Lando was eyeing a beautiful knotted branch in a mottled grey and brown bark.

"Dada wants to carve that into a special walking stick," Silole replied.

"Why special?" he asked.

"He calls it a ceremonial stick; but I can give you this." She gave him a ripe guava that had just dropped off from the tree in the yard.

Suddenly she heard Aunty Mina calling her name from the house.

"Miri! Miri! Silole! Please wash your hands and come to the table immediately! Dinner is ready. You will have to eat it cold." Her aunt did not like to be kept waiting.

"I must go in now. I'll not be allowed out after supper," Silole said. "Shall we meet tomorrow?"

"Yes, but I must ask my father." Lando replied. "We may not be here. We're going on safari to Kericho. I wish I was staying here instead. I like you."

Silole heard car doors being slammed shut, the purr of the engine grow into a throb, and saw the beam of the headlights pull away from her window, plunging the room into darkness. She smiled happily to herself; even though Lando had gone, it had been a nice day. She liked Lando. Maybe he would come back and decide to live in Nakuru forever, so they could become really good friends. That was bound to make her sisters jealous. Silole lay back in bed, listening for sounds above the drumming of the raindrops. Doris was snoring gently. A dog barked somewhere; maybe it was barking at the car. She snuggled back into her blanket and held it tight around her.

(1960)

Maryanne's journey to Nairobi was almost boring for her. She had often travelled the distance from Nakuru to Nairobi by train, at least from about the age of seven. That's when she was enrolled at the boarding school at Mangu, near Thika, run by Roman Catholic nuns. They had told her she had a better chance of getting a job one day with an English-sounding name instead of Silole. She could remember details of every trip since then. She found it strange that she could not recall much about her life when she was younger, except isolated incidents. Harry, a close friend of Rodney Hutchison, 'Uncle Hutch' in Kitale, greeted her at the station. She recognized Harry from a small black and white photograph that her real mother had given her when she was in Form Two. He extended a strong sunburnt hairy hand in greeting as she stepped carefully across the gap between the train and the edge of the platform.

"Be careful here, my dear. Welcome to our beautiful garden city," he said, with a broad smile. "I guess this is going to be your new home for a while."

"I guess so," Maryanne smiled warmly. "Thank you ever so much for meeting me." She said, "Uncle Hutch described you so

well. He even mentioned that scar on the left side of your face."

Harry self-consciously put his hand to his face. "Oh that! That's what you get if you try to be nice to a female cheetah without asking her permission. It will be forty years next month since she did that to me." He seemed to be relishing a distant memory. Maryanne changed the subject abruptly to his dog; she knew to be cautious with men who spoke sentences with a possible double meaning.

"What a beautiful dog," Maryanne said, careful not to stroke the animal. It was common knowledge that almost all dogs in Kenya were trained solely to savage strangers, especially if they were darker-skinned than their owners. Harry loaded her single case and a worn duffle bag into the Austin Forty, and they headed for the Women's Residence on the Hill behind Saint Andrew's Kirk. Harry recited a litany of trivia about Nairobi from the *Muzungu* (European) point of view, most of which Maryanne let enter in one ear and out of the other. She wondered how her life was going to change. She had never imagined even making it to college. Now she was determined to do her best and excel at everything, as she had done at Mangu.

"Here we are," Harry said as he pulled up at the entrance. He held open the door as Maryanne alighted. He carried her bags into the lobby and left her a paper with a scribbled contact phone and the name of his live-in companion, Nancy.

"Fare thee well, dear one. Please telephone me in a couple of days with all your co-ordinates. Nancy and I would simply love to get you up to our little *shamba* (farm) at Tigoni," he said as he shook her hand and, with dog, departed. Maryanne was now alone.

Registration was a straightforward process. One of two clerks from the Registrar's office glanced at her copy of the Acceptance Letter and her birth certificate, Maryanne Hunter-Brooke. That evening there was a big welcome dinner for the new students. Miss Waterbury, the Matron of the Women's Halls of Residence, or Women's Dorm as it was better known, welcomed the girls. She spoke passionately of the responsibilities of each one of the students to themselves and their fellow residents, and to society at large, as they embarked on their journey together into a brave new world. "You are especially privileged. Today, in much of the under-developed world, girls are not even allowed to attend primary school," Miss Waterbury said. "Who in Kenya would have dreamt, even five years ago, that students of all races could learn, play, and live together under one roof—equals in an unequal world? As you

walk through these portals when your short stay with us is over, each of you must reflect on what you have brought to these Halls of Residence, and what you are taking away. You must all leave with a sense that the experience you gained here has enriched you more than all the wealth of the world. You must reflect on how you, in turn, will share this wealth to make Kenya, Uganda, Tanganyika, and Zanzibar, each a better country for your countrymen and women," she continued for a few moments, and then abruptly said, "Oh dear, I have ambled for too long… so, my dear girls and friends, Welcome! *Karibuni!*"

Maryanne looked around in awe. Miss Waterbury was right. There were girls of all races in the room. She had never been in such a mix before. At Mangu they were mainly African girls in the early years. Then they built a new school for mixed-race children and a few Goan and Seychellois girls. The nuns would only accept Catholics. She looked across the room. There were many African girls and three Europeans. She could tell the group of Goan girls at the far end. Maryanne was proud that she could tell the differences among the various Asian looking people. She had learned that from Dada, who, with Aunty Nina, ran the home in Nakuru where she spent her school holidays. Dada had lectured her when she was thirteen. "They are as different as Italians and Englishmen or Germans, so learn to tell the difference, he had said severely." She could now easily identify between the Gujarati, Ismailis, Sikhs, Punjabis, and Pakistanis. Her colleague waved to someone two tables away, also called Mary — what a coincidence, Maryanne thought. The girl looked Seychellois.

Miss Waterbury stood up and left the room. This triggered a pandemonium. She heard someone scream her name.

"Mary! Mary! Maryanne, is that you? You have changed your hairstyle!" Joyce and her three colleagues, Cynthia, Dahlia, and Violet, had also been at Mangu, albeit in different years. Maryanne was very happy to see familiar faces. She had been dreading starting life at college without knowing a soul. It was a joyous reunion as they caught up on each other's stories. The other girls started leaving the dining room as it neared lock-up time. The lights were turned off and on again to dim. The five girls moved into the student lounge and carried on chatting for another hour or so before turning in for the night. Outside the lounge, they paused by the bulletin Board to look at photos from the last end-of-term dance. They pointed each other out and some of the other girls in the dorm. The names did not

mean much to Maryanne. They pointed out boys' faces and linked them to some girls.

"Antoinette is the Women's Hockey captain, and that one's hers. Euréma is the Women's Table Tennis captain. She's very good, better than most men. This boy goes with her, but I don't think it'll last. "G" is also dating this one, but its top secret." The girls giggled. They loved sharing top secrets.

"By the way, Maryanne, look, but do not touch, until you get the OK from us. We'll tear you apart if you steal anyone's boyfriend. We are loyal to each other, and attack like a pack of hyenas, if threatened!" Joyce said. Then, like giggling high school girls, they dispersed into their respective rooms. Maryanne went to bed happy that night. Everything and everyone had been perfect. She tucked herself snugly under the blanket and closed her eyes. A thought crossed her mind. Antoinette's boyfriend in that photo looked vaguely familiar. She was very tired. She quickly fell into a deep sleep.

PIECES OF TIME
by Lisabeth Neuman

THE SCENT OF LAVENDER overwhelmed her — her grand-mother's scent. It hung heavily in the air, even though Gran was gone. Lily was home for the last time.

She tried to hold back her tears, but couldn't stop them anymore. She sat at the big harvest table, facing the old gas stove. No more savoury aromas, no more stories, and no more tea from it. Lily felt alone.

Her throat raw, and feeling breathless, the sudden scratching at the door startled her. She stood to open it.

"Daphne," she exclaimed to the old tortoise shell cat that came in howling with displeasure. "Hey old girl, where have you been?" The cat jumped up on the counter and continued complaining. "I miss her too, Daffy. Let's see if Gran left any food for you."

Lily rumbled around in the cupboards. She found some cans of tuna and she served the still- complaining animal. Great, she thought, one more thing to deal with.

She wandered around the kitchen touching the knickknacks that had become so familiar to her. She felt weary.

She heard a car in the driveway and went outside to find her ex-husband and children pull up. She ran to greet their chubby little arms, silently agreeing with herself to kill her ex-husband.

"Hi you guys. I didn't expect to see you here."

"We didn't want you to be lonely." Jonah gave her a big toothless grin.

"Mommy," Caroline tugged at her sleeve. "Guess what daddy got us?"

"I don't know Sweetie."

"A doggy!"

Lily looked up to see a huge grey wolf running towards her. The animal jumped up on her chest and licked her face.

"Gloria, get down." Jonah pushed at the beast with his tiny hands.

"Jason," Lily yelled, "what is going on?"

"It's alright mommy, Gloria's a good girl." Lily looked down into her daughter's big brown eyes. She pushed the wolf away as Jason ambled over.

"Hi Lil. I'm sorry about Gran."

"What's going on?"

"We didn't want you to be alone."

"Jason, I can't deal with the kids right now. The funeral is tomorrow, they should be in school and..."

"Lily, it's okay. They're in kindergarten. How much circle time do they need?"

"Oh, and what does Heather think about this?" Lily couldn't hold the snarl.

"Come on Lily, let's not start. Would you just once in your life let me try to do something nice for you?"

She blew out a breath. "Jason, what am I supposed to do with the kids? I really need you to take them for the next few days, somewhere else."

"Lily, we're..." he looked toward the house where barking was heard, followed by a crash.

A headache started behind her eyes. "There's a wolf in the house Jason."

"She's a German Shepherd, Lily." More crashing sounds came from the house.

The familiar anger returned to her. "Jason, this is not what I need right now."

Lily stormed into the house. The kitchen looked fine. In the

dining room, the cat was on top of the china cabinet and Gloria was barking her way to oblivion. Two vases lay broken on the floor.

"I'll clean it up Lily."

Without another word to Jason, Lily stomped off to the kitchen, made tea and took it outside, hoping it would calm her. Although not exactly a farm, it was a good-sized piece of property. She had neighbours, but they weren't in your back pocket — the one thing she missed most about living in the city.

Lily sat on the porch step, put her tea beside her, and pulled out the envelope she had found in her Grandmother's desk.

My Dearest Esther,

I am enclosing the ring I gave you. Please don't send it back to me. As much as I love you, I know you have to stay with Tom. I know how important it is to you to keep him at home, since the stroke. Much as it hurts me, I love you all the more for it.

I treasure the moments we had, and I will always think of you with love. Our pieces of time, I will treasure always.

I am moving to Winnipeg to be closer to my daughter. Please don't feel sorry, I have Eleanor, just as you have Lily. I know you are proud of her and you have done a fine job raising that girl since her parents died.

I wish the best for you my love. You will forever be in my heart.

Alton.

Lily removed the emerald ring from the envelope, and watched how the sunlight played with the sparkling colours. She heard laughter from her children through the open window. She was happy *they* were here. Draining her tea, she put the ring and letter back into her pocket and went into the house.

Jason was watching television. Jonah and Caroline were on the floor trying to play a game of cards without much luck. Gloria was trying to eat the cards. Daphne glared from the top of a bookcase.

"How about dinner?" Lily asked when she entered the family room.

"Yes, yes, yes."

"I'll help," Jason offered.

"It's okay. I can handle dinner."

Jason ignored her and followed her into the kitchen.

"Hey Lily, let's go into town and get some pizza or burgers. I know you don't feel like cooking."

"Because Caroline will want burgers and Jonah will want pizza and I'm not up to listening to them bicker. I needed some peace and quiet. Remember? That's why the kids were supposed to be with you." Jason sighed and ran his hands through his shaggy blonde hair.

"Okay, then at least let me make dinner."

"Thanks but making dinner will give me something to do. Just don't expect anything fancy." She reached into the cupboard and pulled out a couple of boxes, then pulled a package out of the freezer.

"Brilliant Lil, mac'n cheese and hotdogs." Jason laughed.

"Yup, comfort food. Even I need it sometimes." Lily's eyes moistened.

"Lily..." Jason made a move to embrace her, but she pushed him away.

"Just let me make dinner."

Lily and Jason sat on the porch swing after the children were tucked in for the night. One slept with the dog, the other with the cat.

"Gran had an affair."

"She *did*?"

"Yeah, after Granddad had his stroke and I was in university. I'm in shock."

"She's still your Gran, Lil."

"She feels so unfamiliar right now – like I don't know who she was."

"Lily, you can't line people up the way you do with numbers in your columns."

"Well, you can't always just paint over what you don't like."

"I don't, I paint what I see and what I like."

"Oh, you mean like Heather's tits."

"Yeah. Yours too."

Jason put his arm around her and drew her close. He felt familiar, but she didn't want him to. Her head went to his shoulder anyway.

"She was your Gran Lily, but she was still a human being. If she had an affair, it was none of your business. It's still none of your business."

"You mean like your affair was none of my business?" She pulled away from him.

"You left me. We weren't together so yeah, it was none of your business." Jason let her think for a few minutes. "After your Granddad's stroke, he gave up. She looked after him, you, and this house. You should be thrilled she found some happiness for herself. She was entitled to it. She wanted you to have your life and wouldn't have asked you to come home. She was a wonderful woman."

"Yeah, she was. She never liked you much though."

"Not true. She just didn't think I could support you and the kids."

"She didn't think you would be able to take care of me."

"Well, I guess she was right about that."

"I'm sorry Jason, really I am. I didn't mean it the way it sounded."

He looked at her. "Why did we fall apart Lily?"

"I'm not tidy and it drove you crazy."

"We could have gotten a housekeeper."

"I hated the smell of your oil paint."

"I could have switched to acrylic."

"Oh Jason, I love your work, but the starving artist thing wasn't for me."

"Lil, I'm not a starving artist. I have my portrait business and it affords me tons of opportunity for gallery work."

"Selling naked paintings of Heather?" Her snarl was back.

"Yeah, I sold the paintings I did of Heather, but not yours. Every time I display one of your paintings, there's a "not for sale" sticker right beside it. Heather and I split up. We're not together anymore."

Lily sulked. "You always painted my thighs too fat."

"I love your thighs."

"I hate them."

"We're not what we were, Lily. I meant what I said about Heather. It's over."

"Congratulations." She was being a bitch and knew it.

"Jesus, Lily. When did you get to be such a wet blanket? You excelled in fine arts and then turned yourself into a cranky bookkeeper. You're no fun and you don't have any fun. Do you remember how? Life is more than a balance sheet. Your Gran knew it. Live it up a little, even if it's not with me. Human beings get lonely. She was lonely. Don't you ever feel that way?"

"It's different now."

"Yeah it is different now. We're both grown-ups."

"This isn't the time. I'm burying my grandmother tomorrow."

"Maybe that makes it the perfect time to ask you."

"Ask me what?"

"Will you go out with me?"

"What?"

"Will you go on a date with me?"

"Jason, I'm tired, I'm going to bed."

"I'll always be here for you, Lily."

Lily went to bed, annoyed, sad and lonely.

She was happy they were there, even Jason; especially Jason.

After the funeral, as they tidied up the kitchen. There was a knock on the door. Lily opened the door to a handsome older man. His full head of snow-white hair fell past the collar of his shirt, his eyes, deep pewter grey.

"I hope I'm not intruding. My name is Alton Redmond." Lily froze. Jason was at her side in an instant, extending his hand.

"How do you do Mr. Redmond, I am Jason Munro, Lily's husband – ex-husband."

"Hello. I wanted to give you my condolences, Lily. I know how much your Gran meant to you."

There was an uncomfortable silence. Lily broke it. "How often did you see my grandmother?"

"Lily!" Jason hissed.

"It's all right, Jason. Please come in and sit down." Lily sat down beside the older man, Jason across from him. "I know about your relationship with my Grandmother. I found a letter."

Alton's eyes started to water and Lily smiled.

"It's okay, Mr. Redmond."

He pulled out a handkerchief and wiped at his tears. "Please, call me Alton." He paused and took a breath. "I was selfish. Your Granddad was sick. My wife died before I met Esther. We met at the library one day and became friends. Your Gran still had your Granddad to look after, but I wanted her to be with me. She wouldn't leave your Granddad. I moved to Winnipeg. It hurt too much to see her and not be with her."

"I know, Alton," Lily said gently.

"There was a ring."

"Yes, I'll get it for you."

"No, no. I bought it for Esther and I want you to have it."

"Gran cared about you, Alton. I know she did."

"You do?"

"She kept your letter and ring."

Alton wiped his tears. "I've got to go."

Lily gave him a hug. "Thank you, Alton."

After Alton left, Jason and Lily sat at the kitchen table.

"I think I'm going to be heading off soon, Lily," Jason said. "I've got a sitting tomorrow morning."

"With Heather?" She raised her eyebrows.

Jason laughed, "No, with some guy named Ivan." He looked at her seriously. "I meant what I said."

"About what?"

"I want to take you on a date when you get home."

Lily smiled. "Okay Jason, I'd like that."

Lily detected a faint smell of lavender in the air. It was good.

CANOES
by Gordon W. Pannell

NOW IN 2009, I'M at that time in life and storytelling that I can confess to being an accomplice to a theft. Not the first one in my life, but the biggest. I will tell everything that lead up to that crime.

Back in 1945, that is 64 years ago, I got a summer job at Blue Ribbon. Blue Ribbon packaged coffee, chocolate and peanut butter. I had wanted a job in a factory. I had worked at Loblaws part-time for a few years while I was going to high school. One Christmas, I worked at a shoe store where I almost outdid the manager in selling slippers and now I wanted to work in a factory.

Once, at the Blue Ribbon, I was asked to get a left-handed monkey wrench from the basement. I acted dumb and asked how was I supposed to get down there?

"Use the elevator." Down I went to the maintenance man and filled him in. I asked him to show me the furnace and the workings of the basement. He helped me get a wheelbarrow and we loaded it up with pipes and everything that would go into it. Now this took about an hour and a half. I was enjoying myself because I knew what was going to happen when I got back to the floor where I was supposed to be working.

"Guy down there wasn't sure what you guys wanted so he gave me all this stuff. Is this what you want?"

The floor manager was there when I got back and the guy who sent me down got into big trouble. All the ladies operating the canning machines smiled and looked at me and shook their heads.

There is a "Dodger" in every story and so it was at Blue Ribbon too. This little street urchin was there to lead us good little boys astray. Ahem! He tried to get me to sell ties. I would work for a pittance while he made a lot? I don't think so.

He had a great idea. We would "borrow" two canoes and go sail Lake Ontario. At seventeen, I believed this. He would steal a canoe at the Credit River and paddle it up to Centre Island. Another guy would get one from the local lagoon. I would get a sail, another kid would get a mast and boards, then all we had to do was lash the two canoes together and presto, we had a catamaran, ready to sail off into the wild unknown. Believe me, you really had to be seventeen to go for this nonsense. We believed. Hell! We could have gone off to war believing that we would come back.

We snuck over to Centre Island and lashed the two canoes together. They had been hidden somewhere. I was the "lasher". I masterly created our sea-going ship using my great knowledge of shipbuilding that I had gleaned from turning a skiff (actually it was a punt but how many people would know what a punt was) into sailboat the year before at Cooks Lake.

With stolen paddles we headed out, six of us, through the eastern gape of the Toronto harbour, into Lake Ontario. At least Columbus had some navigational skills. I haven't the slightest notion where we thought we were going but the wind sure as hell did. No sooner had we cleared the gape than we were gone. I thought the expression was "Go West young man Go West." Not so. Off we went down Lake Ontario to God knows where and at that moment, He wasn't telling us.

"East my hearties and hang on to what? I don't know." No life jackets, a sail that would go only one way and no rudder except our paddles.

The waves were three feet high and we were screaming east at who knows how many miles an hour? The waves were six inches over our gunwale. One of the boys couldn't swim. Terrified, he sat in the bottom of our canoe crying. He felt sure he'd drown. I told him, "Shut up and keep bailing." Horatio at the helm.

Because we were traveling with the wind, the waves were

running with us. We paddled like crazy, trying to stay in a trough. Miles ahead we could see Scarborough Bluffs. We paddled like hell. Wimpy, in the middle, bawled like hell. After about another hour of terror, we hit the beach. At the bottom of the bluffs, we were grounded, with three-foot waves coming at us. We could do nothing but accept our fate.

Here we were, late in the afternoon, miles from where we started. No dry clothes, no food, at the bottom of a cliff we didn't know we could climb. We had our asses whipped. I dug a shallow grave in the sand and went to sleep. I woke cold and stiff in the morning, with a long walk ahead and a "I hope no one finds out about this" to haunt me for the rest of my life. Did we learn anything? Maybe?

And my wife wonders why I don't want a canoe.

An excerpt from the novel
HOT SUMMER
by Judy Powell

DERRICK DROVE ALONG A road which, in Summer's mind, was way too narrow in some places. Still, it was a pleasant ride. She enjoyed the greenery, and especially going through the small towns where people would be going about their daily business. To Summer, the trip was an eye-opener.

When she saw a man riding a donkey with two huge baskets hanging on either side, she got excited and Derrick laughed at her all over again. "The man's going to do his work. He's a farmer. That's how he gets around."

"I know. I'm not that stupid. But it's just that you don't see these things every day. At least, I don't. Not in Chicago. I like seeing all this new stuff. I mean, it's different. You have to understand, I'm doing studies in Communications. All this is stuff I can use in my work. Don't you see?"

"Whatever you say," he said, smiling.

Almost forty minutes later they arrived in Linstead. They turned off the main road and onto a narrow track that led to a small house almost hidden by trees. Derrick drove into the yard and

immediately three dogs rushed out, barking madly.

A stout black woman ran around from the back of the house, shouting, "Rex, Prince, get out of here. Go on." She picked up some small stones and threw them at the dogs. "Lady, go look after your puppies."

She broke a switch from the shrubbery and hit them on the rump. They dashed away, still barking. She bent to pick up her hat, which had fallen off in the flurry of activity and, with a broad smile on her face, approached the vehicle.

"Well, finally, Mr. Dunn. Courtney called and told me you coming so I was looking out for you over two hours now. What happen?"

"Traffic backed up on the road, Mrs. Kitson."

She peered into the vehicle. "And this is the nice lady who is going to do the interview?"

Derrick nodded. "Yes, this is Summer Jones."

"Welcome to Linstead, Mam," she said, smiling, and took the hand that Summer stretched to her in greeting.

Derrick and Summer got out of the vehicle and walked with her up the pathway to the little blue house.

"I was planning to prepare breakfast but when it gets so late and I don't see you, I change my plan. I am going' work on lunch instead. " She wiped her hands on her apron. "I was jus' aroun' the back trying to catch the chicken but it give me quite a chase, you see."

"Why were you chasing a chicken?"   Summer asked, confused.

"For lunch." Mrs. Kitson looked at her as if she should have known.

"But you can't kill a chicken now."

"Why not? You don't eat chicken?" She looked perplexed then nodded as if in realization. "Oh, you are vegetarian."

"No," Summer said, feeling a little stupid. "It's just..."

"Good," the woman cut in. "You too skinny to be vegetarian. You need some meat on your bones. Come on to the back with me. Let's get a nice, big one and I'll cook a sweet lunch for you."

Before Summer could say another word, Mrs. Kitson grabbed her by the arm and dragged her off to the back of the yard with Derrick in tow. As they walked, the woman kept up a constant chatter.

"I tell the little boy from next door to catch one for me, you

know, but him been running around the yard and not catching a thing, not even fly. Anyway, make we see what him up to."

They walked along the dirt path to the back of the house just in time to see a small boy, no older than eleven years old, holding a chicken down on the ground with a metal basin covering its body, its head and neck exposed. The chicken was flapping violently under the basin and squawking wildly.

He had a large knife in his hand and was just about to swing it down onto the bird's neck when Summer screamed.

"Stop! Leave that chicken alone!"

The boy stopped, his eyes wide, then got up from his knees and backed away. Summer ran towards him knowing she must have looked like a mad woman but she didn't care. She grabbed the basin off the chicken. It flapped wildly and flew off into the bushes.

"But what you doing?" the woman exclaimed, indignant. "That was your lunch."

"It's okay," Summer said, panting, "I don't need any lunch. I'm fine. Just leave the chicken alone. Please."

"Well," the woman said, shaking her head in obvious frustration, "if that's what you want you want. But I don't see how can come into my house and I don't give you something to eat. The only other thing I can offer you is some soup."

"Yes," Summer said, relieved. "Soup would be fine."

"Alright." She turned to the boy. "Orville, go light the fire under the pot with the goat head soup. Quick, quick." She turned to Summer. "It won't take long — just ten minutes to heat it up."

"Goat head... soup?" Summer asked, feeling her stomach go queasy. "Ah, thank you, but it's okay. I'm really not hungry."

"Not even a little of the soup?" The woman almost looked offended.

"Mrs. Kitson, I thank you so much for your offer," Summer said quickly, in an effort to appease her, "but I'm fine."

"Alright, Mam." The woman sighed. "You are a strange one to come to somebody's house and want to go away on an empty stomach but, if that is what you want..." She put her hands up as if in resignation.

Derrick smiled and put his arm around the woman's shoulders. "Mrs. Kitson, it's okay. We're in a hurry right now but next time we pass through we'll stop and eat. I promise."

SNIP

by Sylvia Price

THERE IS A MAN lying on her bed. Tori screams, but it comes out too thin and papery for anyone to hear. She should turn and run but indignation chokes good sense. Her things are here and she is damned if she'll abandon them. She eyes her cell phone lying useless on top of the desk. If she goes for it, he will reach it first. She remembers the panic button and makes a quick move towards it but then she realizes it is Ben on her bed.

She spent dinner flirting with him. Delighted by her new-found boldness and the warmth of his reception, she let him fondle her knee under the table. He took that as invitation and that was her fault. She never learned the unspoken language that passes between men and women.

She tries to channel Monique. After three years in university residence, Monique assures her she knows everything about the dealings of men and women. This morning Tori resolves to be more like Monique but the truth is she will never be anything but dull, simple Victoria Ethridge who has no idea what to do with this man in her bed. She'll practice. This is what Monique has advised.

Ben ignores her scream, hands clasped behind his head, he

smiles at her. She smiles back.

"Sit down Tori." He pats a spot beside him.

But Tori takes a step back. She could pull the alarm. She should pull the alarm. But she does not pull the alarm. Her fear is not temptation or danger; her fear is that she will do what is safe. It taunts her and calls her like sin calls the sinner. She'd like to be a sinner. She twists her hands into her pockets and forces herself to meet his gaze.

"Why are you here?"

It's a little girl's question. Ben laughs at her and crosses his ankles. He pats the spot beside him again.

Leo called her a silly little girl just before he stole her car. She is still angry about that car. It was a complete write-off and she was more upset over that than over Leo. Before she could make an idiot of herself, Monique dragged her off and they got matching tattoos, and then she had something to steady her. She smiled all through the funeral thinking about the little black rose on her right shoulder.

She looks at Ben on her bed and shakes her head. Did she intend this? She told Monique she wanted to start anew. Would it be wrong to sleep with Ben just for the fun of it? Other people do it all the time. She wants to be like other people.

"Do you want me to leave?" Ben asks.

In answer, she shrugs off her jacket and turns to show him the tattoo. Ben's eyes skim her bare shoulders and his gaze feels good. She has been alone since Leo died. She wants someone who did not know him. She wants someone who will not ask why he was driving so fast. She wants someone who will not wonder out loud why he was driving with a suspended license. She wants someone who will not blame her. She wants to stop blaming herself. She lets her shoulders droop and defeat settle around her.

"I'm tired Ben. You should go." She moves for the alarm. She does not want to be the predictable Tori Ethridge but it's the only role she knows. She hesitates.

Leo's photo is propped up with her other pictures. He has that little satisfied smile on his face that says he is full of secrets he will not share. She's never had secrets.

Ben pats the spot next to him. It might turn out that he is as complicated and difficult as Leo but she does not think so. It's not as if she has to marry him.

Her eyes shift to Monique's picture. Monique's eyes are

narrowed for the camera. She says that last argument was Leo's fault. She says the accident was his fault. She says Tori has to stop accepting responsibility his idiocy.

Monique is right. Here, in this new place, what has been hazy becomes suddenly clear. She takes a deep breath and sits down beside Ben. He pats her bottom sending a swirl of heat spiralling up into her throat.

"That's my girl," he says.

"I hardly know you."

"So we'll get acquainted," he walks his fingers up her spine. Tori wiggles back into the curve of his body and sighs. "I knew I liked you when I heard you hammering in nails for pictures. You aren't supposed to do that. I got shit for it."

"For the money we pay, I think we're entitled."

Ben laughs as if it is the cleverest thing anyone has said and Tori preens in his admiration. He traces the outline of her tattoo.

"You are a bit of a rebel aren't you?"

Tori laughs out loud. She is a rebel, yes she is. She doesn't care if it is a line to get her into bed. She doesn't care if he's only using her. She intends to use him. She can be anything in this place where no one knows her. She can be Monique with her wild hair and blood red lips.

Ben loops an arm about her waist.

"I like your laugh."

"I might scream again." But her voice is teasing. She pouts at him the way she thinks Monique would.

"You will if you let me stay," he promises and Tori turns red everywhere.

Ben sits up and nuzzles her neck. He is a little unsteady and that makes her giggle. But doubt creeps back. She and Leo were together for so long. She squeezes her eyes shut and pulls away.

"It's too soon," she says and gets off the bed. The alarm beckons her, siren like. She keeps her eyes shut.

"How long since he died?" Ben is resigned.

"Three months."

"It is not very long," he agrees. "But you have to live best you can. There is no harm in a little fun."

He's right, she is sure he is. She wants him to be. She'd like to have fun. She does not want to use that alarm no matter what it is insisting.

"I'm still so shaken from his death I can't possibly know

what I want."

"A girl with a tattoo knows exactly what she wants," says Ben.

She opens her eyes and looks into Ben's face. He's right.

I have a boyfriend, she will say to Monique.

Her heart is beating so hard it smashes against her ribs making it hard to get deep breaths. Heat floods her to the fingertips. She takes a step towards Ben. Yes, yes, she can change.

"Mr. Sinclair, what are you doing bothering poor Mrs. Ethridge?" The door bursts open and in bustles Marcia.

"Busted," groans Ben.

Tori snatches her jacket from the chair back and pulls it about her shoulders. She cannot look at Marcia, a woman who favours a hair colour nature did not intend. She is wearing a dreadful cotton tunic printed with teddy bears. Tori finds it insulting.

"You should have rung," Marcia clicks her tongue against the roof her mouth. "Didn't anyone show you the bell?" She points at the cord. "You ring if he comes back in here. You ring. Come along now Mr. Sinclair."

"Tori and I were getting better acquainted," Ben tells her.

"I'll just bet you were. You watch this one. He's a randy old goat." Marcia eyes Ben with affection and slaps his hand as it begins to reach for her bottom. This does not bother Tori. She understands Ben's only motivation is frustration.

Marcia herds Ben out of the room, cheerfully ignoring his curses. Tori's heart clenches. Disappointment drives at her like hail at peony blossoms.

She looks at the picture of her granddaughter and makes herself smile. She puts a hand to her shoulder where the little black rose sits and stares at the cord she ought to have pulled. Good behaviour is assumed of her here, as it has been all her life.

"It is never too late to change," Monique would say.

Tori gets out her sewing shears. It has taken eighty-two years but she is done with self- doubt. She is done with being good.

Ben is back an hour later, grinning and chortling just as she hoped he might me. He closes the door quietly.

"The witch's shift is over."

And Tori holds up the alarm cord neatly snipped in two and pats the spot beside her.

THE HEIRLOOM
by Elana Rae

I WAS IN MY early teens when Mother began her love affair with the gun. She wasn't raised on a farm, wasn't a hunter, and on the surface of things lived a traditional life as wife and mother. But the glint in the half-dazed eyes, the gleeful smile of anticipation as her hand reached for the drawer that held the gun, left no doubt about her passion. She'd had brief flings before with a hunting knife. The hatchet she liked to bury in closed doors that kept her from her favourite prey—my father, and her hands, themselves weapons of destruction; but I have to say it was the gun that fuelled her.

As with many love affairs, it started by accident, incidental to daily life. The gun was borrowed. Dad operated a small business as an extra investment, and often brought home large amounts of cash, leaving him vulnerable to thievery and attack so his friend Max loaned us his gun for protection. How comforting it would have been if the danger was really out there, but for us it lurked within.

My older brother James had a 22-calibre rifle he used to hunt squirrels. His victims were skinned, their fur tacked to a board in the basement to dry. Mother was discriminating though; she had no interest in the rifle. The one she loved was Max's sleek, grey Smith

& Wesson revolver — a six-shooter.

Each of us had our treasured mother with the gun story, and we dragged them out periodically like other families did their albums. Dad's favourite is the one where Mother would rise up from their bed in the middle of the night, slowly open their bedside table drawer, and draw the gun out. A venerable storyteller himself, Dad provided us with the in-depth details of the crazed look on Mother's face as she fondled the gun. Ever so gently, Dad would bring her back from her drunken stupor enough to retrieve the gun.

James by far was the biggest threat to mother's tyranny, as he was the only one who could on occasion control her. Perhaps that was one of the attractions of the gun — the contained power of it. All it would take is a light but steady pressure on the trigger and poof, problem eliminated and her rule restored. It must have been tempting.

James occupied a place of honour with respect to the gun. When Mother's middle-of-the-night forays with the gun drawer were happening too frequently, Dad became worried that James would become her primary target. His worry turned to conviction the beautiful day in May when Mother drove downtown to pick me up at the bus stop after work. On the way home, unbeknownst to me, she stopped at a pay phone, dialled our number, and told Linda that she had the gun and she was going to get me. Linda quickly spread the word to James and my father, who searched the house and found the gun. Once their pulse and breathing returned to normal, Dad gave the gun to James to hide in a place where only he would know of its location. James must have felt important to be named the "keeper of the gun".

Linda doesn't remember her gun story but my husband Darrin does and he loves to tell it. I had already escaped and left home at an early age, leaving Linda to fend for herself. Darrin was in military officer training and during the summer of our twenty-first birthdays he was stationed in the town where my family lived. I could not leave work to accompany him and on occasion he would drop in to visit and stay with my parents. Linda was sixteen and dating a young man named Mike who was considerably older than her. Mother didn't approve. Late one night I received a call from Derrick. "Your mother's on a rampage. Mike came to see Linda and I was sitting in the TV room in the recliner. Out of nowhere Mike comes running through, followed by your mother chasing him with a gun. She fired over the chair and hit the mirror above the bar. She's crazy."

"Is everybody alright?"

"I guess so. Mike escaped. I'm okay."

For a brief moment I wondered how, when and why the gun was brought out of hiding. Someone must have been careless, desperate or both. Linda doesn't corroborate Darrin's story. But she doesn't deny it either. She just doesn't remember what happened to Mike. He disappeared one day and she always wondered why she never heard from him again.

I never told anyone about my own gun story, until I was safe, miles from home. At mid-life the story is shop-worn, boring to me. I'm loath to repeat it. It was unique in our family though, as I was not usually the brunt of Mother's violence. I tried to disappear, make myself scarce, and keep a low profile. I walked and spoke softly, could be found most often in my bedroom with my books. There I'd escape to worlds where anything was possible. Otherwise, I could be found trying to pacify or please Mother—anything to prevent the monster rising. Mostly I just wanted her to love me.

Dad was also an escape artist and he often slept in his office or on his boat, both of which were equipped with comfortable sleeping arrangements. He preferred to travel lightly, unencumbered with children. My siblings went head-to-head with Mother, challenging, confronting—feeding the monster, so it was a rare occasion that found me alone with her. One Friday, my brother and sister were both away. Mother was drunk and her venomous abuse of Dad reached his tolerance threshold. He found me in my bedroom, and announced that he was going to spend the night in a hotel.

"Don't waste your money Dad. Just go to the boat."

"No, she's really after me this time."

"She's drunk. She won't be able to drive the car. You'll be safe there."

Several moments later, I heard her footsteps coming down the hall. Her guttural, gravely voice preceded her into the room.

"Are you a man or are you a mouse?" I heard one of her favourite refrains together with the slamming of the front door. Mother usually reserved this line exclusively for Dad, and for a second I wondered if she considered us interchangeable somehow.

"I've got a gun and a knife and I'm going to the boat to get your father. Do you want to come?" I tossed the idea around for a moment, and then said.

"No, I'll wait here."

"Fine then."

I tried to keep reading once she left, but I kept circling back to

the beginning of the same paragraph. Scenes interrupted the print, made it impossible to move on. Scene one had my mother dead in a head-on collision. Scene two had my father lifeless over the steering wheel of the boat—a knife sticking out of his back, a bullet hole in his head. Scene three had me calling the police to ask for help, my parents being taken to the police station, pacifying the powers that be, and bringing their anger home to me, the one who had betrayed them.

They were back within the hour—a very long hour—sixty seconds, times sixty—one paragraph. Dad rushed breathless into my room.

"She's got a knife. I'm going to a hotel now."

"Okay, Dad. Go. Hurry up."

Ah, the footsteps, the gravelly voice. For a split second, I wondered. "Is it like a hunger that needs feeding? If she can't get Dad, will anyone do?"

"Are you a chicken or do you want to talk?"

"Sure Mom. I like talking."

Mother's love affair with the gun ended the same time her marriage did. She is over seventy now and lives alone in a retirement home. She suffers; chronic pain that eludes an aetiology or diagnosis; blindness that robs her of her passions, cooking, knitting and reading, but her mind is sound. She has no guns or other weapons, and she doesn't drink much either. Nearly impoverished, Mother's choices are limited, but she does play bridge, and maintains a close relationship with her sister and family. Mom doesn't understand why her son has cut her out of his life. Linda and I haven't the heart to tell her. Distance and time, the great healers, have granted me enough safety to play the dutiful daughter, and to see the frightened angry child at the core of our mother.

We survived. None of us has any bullet holes, stab wounds, or obvious lacerations. But my brain has been rewired like some old hot rod. Sneak a peek if someone near me is angry. You'll see terror run rampant over my face—fleeting and completely involuntary, but irreversible nonetheless. And unless you're a child, please don't try to love me, or get too close. I'll run, or shut down, or create an array of manageable compartments to split you into. After all, love, like anger, can kill.

The gun went with Dad when my parents separated. Eventually he remarried, and shared the gun with his new wife Donna. Last we heard, she took the gun with her when she left—but the memories linger.

ADVENTURES OF A KOKANI BOY
by Maheen A. Rashdi and Karim Bondrey

An excerpt from a biography of Karim Bondrey, including some of his own words about his childhood and his training as a naval cadet, some history of Karachi, his place of birth, and a few final words from his daughter.

KARIM WAS OFFICIALLY REGISTERED as "Abdul Karim Bondrey" when he was born on 16th August 1930 in a small house near the light house on Manora Island in Karachi [Pakistan], where his mother lived with her father, Nana. As with the prevalent practice of the time, his "official" year of birth was noted as 1931 instead of 1930, to make him a year younger for official records. The logic of that practice still baffles the mind!

In 1934, he was taken to Ratnagiri [India], along with his mother, by Nana when he retired from Karachi Port Trust, ending his residence at his official KPT lodgings in Manora. The decision to take Karim and his mother was mainly because Karim's father was mostly away at sea, thus leaving his mother alone with a small child.

Karim's earliest schooling began in a children's Marathi school, perhaps at the age four or five, and at age six he was shifted to a Marathi high school known as Patwardhan High School for Boys, one of the best and well-known in Ratnagiri. Set in a good locality, it was built over a large ground, well spread out, the main building being a double-storey structure. After completing four years of Marathi education classes, he was admitted to First Standard of High School where education was in both English and Marathi.

After about eight years or so, in the winter of 1942, Karim finally returned to his island of birth and what was to be his "seat" of excellence in the future. He was returning with his mother and younger brother, Rahim, from Ratnagiri as his father had ended his extended sea travels and had joined the Karachi Port Trust as a pilot.

The return trip could not have been more thrilling. Their route was via Bombay on a ship called *Englistan*. And when the ship arrived off port at Karachi, it was Karim's father who came to pilot the vessel in.

Village life was all that Karim saw in his early childhood. And, at age six, that was a tough life with stringent routines: walking five kilometres to school every day through unpaved village pathways; no money to buy food on the way home; and after walking for an hour on a rumbling tummy he'd first need to finish chores and then would get some food.

But, while he accepted it all as part of life's great offering, with neither resentment nor any discontent marring his optimism for life, there was always an aspiration to go beyond the rural setting and to build upon the latent streak of finesse in him despite the village backdrop of his dwelling.

His soul was always that of a refined autocrat. But no one would have thought at that early age that this young chap from an inconspicuous village in India would go on to enjoy spending time at the Victoria and Albert Museum in London, England; have caviar for his breakfast; and own a vast collection of the music of Mozart, Bach, or Chopin.

Karim recalls of his childhood: "My first memories are of Bankhindi, my village in the town of Ratnagiri where I lived from age four to age twelve with my Mummy, Nana and Nani (my grandparents), while Daddy was serving on ships at sea. I often saw my Dada (paternal grandfather), too, as he used to come to Ratnagiri and stay with us for a few days. He was quite short and stubby,

white haired, very fair and reddish. He did not sport any beard, but always had a few days' growth on his face. He seemed to have very few teeth. He always wore *lungi* (a wrap-around cloth of cotton) and a short sleeved white *banyaan* (vest). He was a jovial, slow-moving figure, and was used to pinching any one sitting near him while looking the other way. Dada was very fond of me and Mummy.

He was well-read in Quraan and was always called upon to offer *Fateha* and *darood* for any special 'spiritual' occasion. He could write Quraanic verses by heart, too. I remember clearly that he used to write verses from Quraan on dinner plates and saucers in ink of liquid *zafraan* (saffron). After drying out, the plates were stacked in cupboards to be given later to the sick and needy who dissolved the *zafraan* and drank the liquid for *shifa* (wellness).

He often gave plates to Mummy as well (with these verses) which Mummy used to drink—maybe for Daddy's safe keeping out at sea. Unscientific and whimsical as these rituals might sound to the modern mind today, they had their purpose.

For Mummy, who had no other education except her belief in the Almighty to guide her through life, this served as the only assurance for Daddy's safety against the storms and other dangers at sea.

And, after all, there's no denying the powers of the Almighty and which human action might garner HIS sympathy!

But I do remember that when my Dada recited *Fateha* at dinner table it was a long wait for all of us for dinner. Hot food often got cold as *Fateha* was a long affair, and if it would have been cut short I don't think the Almighty would have really minded!"

Karim's family and their ancestors belonged primarily to two villages near Bombay—Zambhari and Saitavda—in the district of Ratnagiri in India, and were from a clan which is popularly known as "Konkani" in Bombay.

Ratnagiri is a town in western India, in Mahārāshtra state, on the Arabian Sea coast south of Mumbai (formerly Bombay). It is the centre of an agricultural area; rice, nuts, coconuts, and fruit are grown nearby. Fishing is a mainstay of its economy, as are iron ore and bauxite mining. It is a popular seaside resort, too, and the seat of a marine biology research station. Ratnagiri was an administrative capital and important port of the Muslim kingdom of Bijāpur, and a fort built during that time overlooks the harbour. Thibaw, the last king of Burma (now Myanmar), was exiled to Ratnagiri for thirty years until his death in 1916.

The two villages, Zambhari and Saitavda, are located about a hundred miles south of Bombay on the coastal belt, and the region is called Konkan—hence the word Konkani for its inhabitants. Zambhari is a smaller village, two miles from Saitavda, a hamlet tucked into the base of a hillock. Both villages are very picturesque, with green farmland all around and situated on the bank of a tributary of the river Savitri, as it winds through the countryside. The river meets the Arabian Sea about thirty miles to the north. Karim's ancestral house, that is, his Dada Eshaq Bondrey's house, used to be (and still is) the end house at Zambhari, built on the edge of a small ravine.

In the year 1947, also the year when united India was divided to create Pakistan, Karim set out on the first independent phase of his career. He joined the cadet training ship *Dufferin*, in Bombay, which was to be his home and institution for three years.

Karim still remembers the hard life. He was always hungry; he would get some biscuits from the tuck shop and a horrible brown stew for lunch or dinner. The fat, dark-skinned Chief Steward, an old Goan, with his huge protruding belly, was a sight that always reminded the cadets of the wealth and well-being he achieved at their cost. While the cadets worked and toiled hard all day long, the measly amount of food they got would only half fill their stomachs. They could not complain to anyone for fear of being punished. If there was a commotion or complaint from the cadets about food, the steward always made sure his side of the story would stick and, while for a few days they would get more food, it would soon revert back to his old meagre portions. What a strong reminder of Dickenson times!

The cadets' daily routine was: holystoning and washing the deck, academic classes, sports, seamanship activities, sailing or pulling boats. There would be one early morning *bazaar* boat, bringing in the steward's daily shopping from Mazagon pier to the ship, either sailing across or rowing a distance of about 1½ miles. Popular games played were football, hockey, swimming, sailing and pulling races, etc. Once or twice a term, picnicking over a weekend at nearby islands, such as Elephanta, was permitted where the cadets visited the caves and saw some age-old paintings.

Karim was an achiever. His first award was a book titled *Admiral Nelson's Life*, given to him for "Best Progress in Remove Class" (second year). Then, in the final annual exams (despite fainting because of extreme stress), he got an extra first class certificate and

came fifth. He would probably have been fourth had it not been for favouritism shown to Pearce, who was from a highly influential Hindu family.

Karim's ambition was to get the top position in all areas but, of course, it was not always possible. And, despite trying his level best to get the top marks in Navigation, in which he was extremely good and which carried the best prize—a sextant—he missed it by a few marks. Instead he got a book of Bernard Shaw for "Best progress," signed by his teacher, which he still keeps in his private library.

From the earliest times, Karachi has been on the maps of mariners. It was on the trading routes of the Arabs, and the Arab navigators of the twelfth century called the place *Ras-al-Karazi* (the Cape of Karazi). It has been mentioned in history books from time to time and known variously as Kaurashi, Qarachi, Crochey, and Kurrachee.

Karachi port, unlike the present day modern port, was only an anchorage where ships anchored just off the southern tip of the island then known as Manhara and now as Manora. The entry further inward was blocked by shallow waters and a sand and stone bar which, by some accounts, extended right across from Manora point to the beach (at Clifton).

By the late eighteenth century, Karachi had grown into a town and an important trading centre. The port became a hub of activities for imports and exports. The Amir of Talpurs, who ruled Sind then, realizing the importance of the port, built a fort on the hillock at the southern end of Manora and placed a garrison to guard the entrance.

In 1838, the British, who were already entrenched in India through the East India Company, wanted Karachi as a trooping station for transporting British forces through Sind en route to Afghanistan. The British had apprehended Russian influence in Afghanistan, and they planned to forestall this by establishing a puppet Kingdom, placing on the throne the son of the then King who had fled to India. They needed a secure passage through Sind and saw Karachi as an ideal trooping station.

Life has a habit of becoming stranger than fiction. These tales from an era past and a world far removed from where I now am seem to me to be picked out of a bestselling saga.

The Don Valley hills surround my apartment building in Toronto, as I recount my father's story beginning with life in a small village in pre-partitioned India. I feel an equal part of two

far removed civilizations. Like the distance that separates them, the extreme cultures I have seen, and read and now written about may be as foreign to each other as extraterrestrials would be to earthlings! But that is not so at all.

This has been a tale of great ambitions, unwavering grit, non-negotiable principles, and, above all, human adaptations.

IN THE DARK
by Pratap Reddy

SHE GOT IN AT the Old Mill station in Toronto, gave a quick glance around the car and then headed to the vacant seat next to him, brushing past his knees. Pulling out a newspaper from her bag, she started to tackle the crossword puzzle. He could smell the Charlie she wore.

He looked at his watch. It was nearing four and the afternoon rush had not yet begun. Its the 14th of August. Tomorrow is his wedding anniversary and he hasn't given a thought about what to give Shalini. Last year he bought her a bouquet of flesh-pink roses and a small bottle of Chanel No. 5.

The girl began to chew the end of her ballpoint pen and continued to wrestle with the clue. He edged closer to her. The side of his thigh touched her lightly. Squinting at the newspaper, he read:

"16. Courtship of the lower extremities, walks that is (7)"

He could feel her knee press against his thigh. Or was he imagining things? He leaned sideways and whispered, "Footsie."

"What?"

"The answer to the clue."

The girl gave him a look and then returned to her crossword.

After filling the last letter, she exclaimed with happiness, "This is the first time I've managed to complete the puzzle!"

"Congratulations!"

"Well, all thanks to you," she said. "Do you like crosswords?"

"Yes, but I don't get the chance to do them."

"Are you too busy?"

"I've plenty of time," he said. "The daily newspaper is a luxury we can't afford. I'm out of job now. What do you do, if I may ask?"

"I'm studying to be a fashion designer."

"Wow! That's really great. By the way, I'm Dev."

"I'm Anne," she said. "Are you from Pakistan?"

"No. India."

"Sorry!"

"Are you from China?"

"No," Anne said. "Laos."

"There we go again!" The lights in the car blinked twice and the train slowed down for no apparent reason. Though it picked up a little speed, it did not breeze into the Yonge Street station the way it usually did.

There was very little light in the station. Nobody rushed to the door to board the train though there were people milling about on the platform. A few of the passengers got off the train, but others continued to sit, looking out of the windows with puzzlement.

An announcer came on the line, "There's a problem with..."

"There's something seriously wrong," Dev said. "Come, let's get off the train!"

"Shouldn't we wait to..."

Somebody in the car said, "Quiet, please."

Dev said, "It's best if we left now. Hurry!"

Anne followed Dev as he bounded out of the train. Soft light filtered down to the platform from the upper levels. They raced up a stalled escalator and squirmed past the turnstile. A group of people had gathered in front of the ticket counter. Anne and Dev took the stairs that led to Yonge Street, ascending like a pair of divers reaching for the surface.

Outside, the scene was amazing. The sidewalks were choked with people. On the road, cars were lined up bumper to bumper. Pedestrians were crossing the roads anywhere and everywhere, sidling between motionless cars.

Dev asked a passerby, "Hey buddy, what's happening?"

"The world's coming to an end, that's what!" said the man, without breaking his stride.

"The traffic lights are not working," said Dev to Anne. "And all the shops look so dark inside."

"I don't see a single cab, anywhere!" said Anne.

"My house is nearby," Dev said. "Why don't you come home with me? Later, you can take a taxi."

"I'd rather not," said Anne. "I want to get home as soon as I can."

"Where do you live?"

"Scarborough," said Anne listlessly.

"Scarborough! That would be one long walk," said Dev.

Anne was silent, as though she was grappling with yet another of her crossword clues.

"I'll have to leave you now," said Dev. "Take care!"

"Wait," said Anne hesitantly. "I hope your place isn't too far away."

"No, not too far," said Dev. "Let's keep talking as we walk, that way you'll not notice the distance,"

"What shall we talk about?"

"For a start," said Dev, "do you miss Laos?"

"I've never been there."

"Were you born in Canada, then?"

"No, in Thailand," said Anne. "My father and mother had to flee Laos."

"During the Pol Pot regime?"

"That's right. My father was a government official and because he was a Royalist, the Pathet Lao were hunting for him. My parents swam across the Mekong one night and eventually made it to Thailand."

"That's some story," said Dev. "Did things get better for your parents in Canada?"

"In some ways, yes. But my father never managed to find a job suited to his education, not knowing English and all that. He died a few years ago. Mom still works as a cleaning lady. How have things worked out for you in Canada?"

"We came to Canada two years ago. We used to live in Dubai," said Dev.

"I've heard of Dubai. Is it in Europe?"

"No, it's in the Middle-East. I worked as a banquet manager in a five star hotel. All the money we brought from Dubai, all those tax-free petro-dollars, it simply evaporated once we came here. We rented

a nice apartment on the Lakeshore and bought a brand new Mazda. We shopped at the best of places. But like your father, I couldn't find a suitable job. One by one, we had to give up everything."

"What about your wife, couldn't she find a job?" asked Anne.

"Our children were very young so she needed to stay at home. Later, she got herself a survival job, but that was only after we sent our children away."

"Sent your children away?" said Anne

"My wife's parents came to visit us last summer. When they were returning to India, they took our children with them so that Shalini could go to work," said Dev.

"It's must be so terrible for your wife... and you!"

"Yeah, it's been bad. Our lives have changed in other ways too. But I'm glad that at least our children are being cared for... We are almost there! My house is only two blocks down the road," said Dev.

"Am I glad to hear that!" said Anne.

"Do you mind if I pick up something?"

They went into a convenience store. The place was jam-packed with people buying things like bread, butter, bottled water and flashlight batteries. Dev picked up a box of strawberry pie.

Dev remembered the day he had asked Shalini to buy a box of strawberry pie from the grocery store. Shalini had been working for three months and he had been laid off from his job at the gas station. Shalini returned from her shopping and dumped a carton of fresh strawberries on the table in from of him. As he looked up in amazement at her, she said: "You should stop eating those disgusting pies. You've put on a lot of weight." Dev couldn't think of a reply.

As they stood in the long line, they heard people talking about the black out.

"I believe that the entire province is without electricity."

"No. All of North America, in fact."

"I'm sure it's the work of terrorists!"

The cash register was not working so the clerk was collecting money and issuing change from a plastic box. They left the store and soon were on the street where Dev lived. The entrance to his basement apartment was in the narrow space between two houses. Dev unlocked the door and stepped inside.

"Isn't your wife at home?" asked Anne.

"No," said Dev, "She's at work, packing undies."

It was almost pitch dark inside. Anne started climbing down

the steep staircase. The door behind her closed by itself. She cried out, "I can't see anything!"

"Here, grab my hand," said Dev. "Ouch! That's not my hand!"

Holding on to each other, they tottered down the steps. When they reached the bottom, Dev bent his head and kissed Anne on the mouth. Anne thought she ought to protest but her lips had a will of their own. Anne felt something hard at her navel. It was the carry-bag containing the box of strawberry pie.

"Stay right here and don't move," said Dev, "while I go and look for a candle."

Dev moved away from her and melted into the shadows. Anne heard the faint sigh of a match, and then golden light bloomed from the kitchen. Dev returned with a candle stuck over an inverted coffee-mug. Dev placed the mug and a knife on the dining table. In the half-light, the furniture around them looked like crouching beasts. As Anne walked up to the table, her own shadow seemed to stalk her menacingly.

Dev went back into the kitchen and returned with a bottle of wine and two wine glasses. He poured each of them a glass.

"Thank you," said Anne as she took the glass and sat at the dining table.

"Let's celebrate!" said Dev. "Today's a very special day."

"What makes you say that? Is it because of the blackout?"

"No, for the first time you've completed a crossword puzzle today."

"Not true," said Anne. "You finished it for me."

"Let me think of another reason. OK, today is *not* my wedding anniversary!"

Anne took a sip of the wine and asked, "How long have you been married?"

"Seven years. Seven l-o-n-g years," said Dev. "What about yourself? You aren't single, are you?"

"Well, at the moment, I am."

"What do you mean by that?"

"I was serious about someone," said Anne. "But it fizzled out."

"That's too bad. What happened?"

"My boyfriend would call me his Annelida," she said. "He was majoring in life sciences. At first, I thought that it was a term of endearment. Need I say anything more?"

"That worm!" said Dev and laughed. Picking up the knife, he cut two slices of the pie and extended the box towards Anne. She selected a piece and took a tentative bite.

"Shalini detests it," said Dev.

Munching the slice of the oversweet pie, Anne said, "I can understand why."

Dev emitted a hollow laugh. He raised the bottle and said, "Would you like to have some more?"

"I'm fine," said Anne.

Dev began to speak wistfully about his life in the Middle-east, of the parties they attended every weekend, of the reckless shopping sprees, and of the long road trips in the desert.

"Can't you go back?" asked Anne.

"You can never really go back," said Dev. "Things change, people change, and Dubai too, I bet."

The airless room had become stuffy and Anne started to feel the beginnings of a headache. The candle had reduced to a stump and tears of wax trickled down the side of the coffee mug.

They heard a scrabbling sound coming from the head of the staircase — as though someone was trying to open the door. Both of them turned to look. The door opened slowly. A shadowy form started climbing down the stairs, but stopped midway. Hard on its heels another shadow appeared, forcing the former to resume its descent.

"You have come back early," said a female voice.

"You too," said Dev, as if he were returning a greeting.

Entering the ring of light, the two figures loomed over the seated pair.

"We seem to have company," said the woman, furtively buttoning her blouse.

"This is my wife, Shalini," said Dev. "This is Anne."

"Hi," said Anne.

"How are you, Raj?" said Dev. "I haven't seen you in ages."

The man wiped his mouth with his hand. He said, "I-I've been busy."

"I can see that," said Dev.

The man giggled. Shalini opened her mouth to speak. But no words came out. The red lipstick she wore was smudged around her mouth. She looked as if she had gorged herself on one of her husband's strawberry pies.

An excerpt from the novel
PERVERSE
by Larry Rodness

"PERVERSE" WAS EMYLINE STIPE'S signature response to almost everything. Others her age were more apt to say "cool" or "wicked" or "awesome." But you knew Emyline was in the room when you heard, "Loved that band last night — so perverse," or "She's hanging with *that* dude? Perverse!" Or, "I hate people who eat with their mouths open or closed or talk when they speak — they're so... perverse."

This was not just an off-hand remark but more an expression of Emyline's mantra, for she was the 18-year-old willowy daughter of Goth parents which made her a rare "second-generation" Goth. Like every teenager, Emyline was trying to figure out exactly where she stood in the world and how to rebel against it.

The trouble with growing up a "second-gen" Goth was that Emyline's parents had already pointed out many of the faults in society's thin veneer leaving very few for her to question on her own. So the conundrum for Emyline was how to rebel against a family of rebels. What would a person in her position do? Become a civil servant or at the very least, an *uncivil* servant?

The first thing Emyline decided to do was leave her parents'

house in the downtown core and move into a second-storey walk-up in a neighbouring district just far enough away to maintain her freedom, but close enough to run home to if need be. To make the rent, she sold cloth in the textile shop downstairs, and for fun she took up with a forty-year-old married man named Harley Brackshire who owned an upscale clothing boutique down the block on the east side. Harley was a tall, slim Brit with a nose so narrow that you could use it to slice open an envelope. The affair was ideal for both of them. For Harley, Emyline was an exotic, forbidden fruit that fed his over-sized ego. For Emyline, this was the kind of doomed relationship she could both, pine and obsess over, to her heart's content.

Life was perfect for almost three weeks until Emyline grew tired of the fling. But being somewhat passive-aggressive, she decided to have Harley end it by making herself so available to him that he'd grow more bored than she. Every day at lunch she'd drop by for a quickie in one of the change rooms and even try to time her trysts with Harley's wife's visits, hoping to embarrass him. To Emyline's surprise however, Harley, misinterpreted her actions as a way to stoke the fires, a tactic which he quite enjoyed. All this sex was cranking up Harley's libido but frustrating Emyline.

Fortunately for one and sadly for the other, it all changed one day when Harley, looking to 'up the ante', suggested they bring in one of his salespeople for a threesome.

This was just what Emyline needed. With melodramatic outrage, she ranted on about how once Goths give themselves to a person it's a sacred bond — or some such bullshit. Harley pleaded and even wept to keep her but the next day, instead of walking east, Emyline walked west. It was a simple enough tactic but the direction life was about to take her next would not be west. It would not be found on any compass at all.

It would begin in a second-hand shop filled with antiques or other people's garbage, depending on one's point of view. The painting sat on the dusty floor, lying flush against the grimy picture window, staring out at Emyline as she passed by like a lost puppy. It was a simple rural winter setting depicting a weathered old wood fence that stretched from the foreground all the way back to a ragged line of trees. The subject of the painting was a lone maple that stood in the pristine snow, exactly halfway between the foreground and the forest. As soon as Emyline saw it she identified with the tree as if she and it were kindred spirits, two figures stranded in a hostile

wasteland. The painting was serene and unsettling at the same time – just the right amount of perversity for Emyline.

She entered the store and immediately sensed an air of malice from the shopkeeper who had worked in the district for over thirty years and had suffered them all — the druggies, the hookers, and the hustlers. He took one look at Emyline and made up his mind before she even said a word: Goths he thought, *if they were so in love with death, why didn't they just kill themselves and let the rest of us get on with our own miserable lives?*

"Hi." said Emyline cheerily. "The picture in the window, the one with the tree, how much?" she asked.

"Says right on it, a hundred and sixty bucks, don't it? You got a hundred and sixty bucks? If not, don't waste my time."

Emyline offered her prettiest smile as she lifted the picture from the floor and eyeballed it like an appraiser from Sotheby's. She quickly reasoned that if he was asking a hundred and sixty dollars, it meant he couldn't have paid more than eighty for it. The heavy line of dust covering the frame also told her it had probably been lying around for at least three or four months, thus the scale was tipping more towards "garbage" than "antique."

"I don't have that much but I'll give you one hundred." she offered.

The shopkeeper, who had been appraising Emyline as closely as Emyline was appraising the painting, cocked his head and with a crooked smile replied,

"Tell you what. You can have her for one hundred dollars— if you do one thing for me."

Emyline knew what was coming next.

"You come back here tomorrow dressed from head to toe in white. You wipe all that black nail polish and that eye shadow guck off, and you come here dressed like..."

"Like a little lady?" asked Emyline.

"Yeah, like that, and she's yours."

Emyline put the picture down where she found it and smiled.

"See you tomorrow then," she sang as she left the shop.

Although she had never met this man before Emyline knew him all too well. Her parents had taught her early on that when people were confronted with something odd or strange they generally went into "fear mode". This man was desperate to prove that he was still in control of his domain and to do that he needed to

demystify Emyline by degrading, exposing, and shaming her into proving that underneath all that Goth guck she was just as dull and ordinary as he was. Emyline knew exactly what to wear.

The next day Emyline returned to the store dressed totally in white, as requested. It was the one white dress she owned and treasured — an exact replica of the bridal gown Miss Lucy was buried in, after Dracula turned her into a vampire. When Emyline entered the shop she looked more frightening in white than anything she had worn in black, and the smarmy look on the store owner's face faded to the same pale shade as the dress.

Emyline approached and slowly opened her hand. The store owner fully expected to find a beating heart pumping away in her pale little palm. Instead there were five twenties.

The owner hesitated a moment wondering whether to deny her the purchase and chase her out, but thought better of it and nervously scooped up the bills. Emyline took the picture and left.

Not a word was said between the two.

Having already picked the spot to hang her prize, Emyline hurried home and opened the front door of her tiny studio apartment to find a single nail in the center of the wall, a nervous bridegroom awaiting its intended. She married the picture to the nail, stepped back to admire their union, and took in the canvas inch by inch, studying every detail from the ruts and grooves of the old wooden fence to the long stretch of pines in the distance. Then at last, she let her eyes settle on the single maple that stood in the centre of the scene and imagined that the painter must have had her in mind when he drew it. The blanket of snow around the tree made everything look peaceful, untouched, and forbidden at the same time. That's when it came to her; something she had instinctively known when she first laid eyes on the painting: there was something more here than just the sum of its parts, something she couldn't quite put her finger on. But then, because even Goths get hungry, she stripped off Miss Lucy's bridal gown and bounced downstairs for a sub.

It was eight-fifteen when she returned, when her world changed, when the glorious mystery revealed itself to her, when she gazed upon her new treasure and noticed for the first time, the footprints in the snow that were not there before!

A PERFECT EVENING
by Philomena Saldanha

AS HE FUMBLED IN his pocket for a lighter, Peter got out of his car and stopped outside his house. He usually crossed the street to the mailbox to get the mail before he went home. His eyes squinting against the glare of the sunlight, he put the cigarette in his mouth and lit it. The first drag worked like magic. His body relaxed and his brow smoothened.

The sun was painting streaks of purple, pink, and gold across the sky as it bade farewell to an ordinary day. The colours of the leaves were turning to vibrant shades of orange, red, purple, and yellow, while still showing some shy greens. The cool evening breeze caressed Peter's face as he stood there quietly hovering in bliss. The moment lasted only as long as his cigarette. As he stubbed his cigarette into the ground, he saw something flash down there. He bent to take a closer look. What was it? A toonie! A shiny toonie! He snagged it and looked furtively around. As he held on to the toonie, he felt a wonderful sense of pride. A perfect complement to this wonderful evening! Losers weepers... finders keepers, his mind cheered. This is precious! The metal of the coin felt good and his fingers lingered with a worshipper's touch. Carefully, he put it

in his wallet. The $100 bills crowding his wallet were mere beggars against the toonie that he had found.

As Peter continued to stroll, he saw a family of skunks walking directly towards him, a mother skunk with three baby skunks. Such beauties, they were dazzling white stripes on luxurious black coats. An incredible urge overcame him. He stopped and lifted the lovely long tail of one of the baby skunks. Before he knew it, mama skunk moved ahead to face him as she sprayed. In perfect cue her three babies sprayed.

"YOU DON'T DO THAT, FOR GOD'S SAKE, ARE YOU CRAZY? THEY ARE SKUNKS," a fat woman let out the most unladylike scream, her face totally contorted. She was straining on her dog leash as she dug in her heels, leaning as far back as she could. The neighbourhood had now been alerted by that scream. The smell of the skunks was beginning to permeate the air rather quickly.

If Peter was aware of the scene he was creating, he did not seem to show it. He held on to the baby skunk's tail in total rapture for another second, while Michael, the neighbour's teenage boy, looked from across the street and laughed, shaking his head, as he said to himself, "Oh Peter, Peter."

Two kids stopped playing ball and watched him. It seemed that all the people on that street had by now turned their heads in Peter's direction, their faces displaying shock and disgust. In a few seconds the ground that Peter was standing on had been transformed into a performing stage, while the spectators had moved away to maintain a healthy distance. But Peter could not have cared less. He scuttled after the skunks and lifted the tail of yet another of the beautiful baby skunks. Mama skunk, now clearly nervous, sprayed yet again and herded her babies to flee from this erratic human behaviour. Peter was smiling from ear to ear, totally delighted as he tried to reach for the last baby skunk to lift its tail. Too late... the skunks had escaped.

Peter was still smiling to himself, as he crossed the street and walked into his garage. He stripped his clothes in the garage, dumped them in a corner, and entered his home in his underwear, wearing the smells of a homecoming warrior. He proudly described to his family his wonderful experience. His mother screamed, "Pedda, you are mad!" Her nose twisting out of joint, she ran to the garage to dispose of his discarded clothes as she screamed, "Where is the tomato juice?"

Her son laughed his head off. His wife was happy; she could not smell anything. Her sinuses being blocked for most of her life seemed like a blessing in disguise. When Peter did not smell of skunks, he smelled like an ashtray or a vomit can.

Peter felt good. He poured himself an indecent shot of brandy and downed it quickly. It had been a perfect evening!

TORN SEAMS
by Mel Sarnese

JULIE LIKED THE SALT-AND-PEPPER-HAIRED man whose phone number and address she found in her missing sister's purse. Julie and Valerie were inseparable as fraternal twins, and were closest friends. When Valerie went missing, and after the police called off the search, Julie took it upon herself to look for her closest confidant. She hunted for clues at her sister's condominium, her work place, and her computer. It was an e-mail that led her to the professor sitting across from her at the tapas bar. He seemed kind, with full, generous lips and mossy green eyes. Julie was puzzled that her sister had never mentioned him to her.

"Thank you for meeting with me. I know my phone call must have seemed strange, but I'm hoping you could help me find my sister," Julie said. "I found your address in her purse. The last time I heard from her was just before she boarded the plane for London."

Ron looked straight into her eyes as he poured her a glass of the dry wine. "I'll try to help you with all the information I know. We met in a chat room and continued our thing online and by telephone for about a month before she came to London to meet me. I wanted to go to Toronto, but she said she had preferred it this way.

We spent a wonderful week together, and I thought we got on well. I was very surprised when she cut off all ties with me upon her return to Canada. She just vanished! I really thought it was her way of telling me to piss off."

"Did she tell you that she was meeting anyone else? Did you drive her to the airport?

She was not on that plane! You must help me find her. Can you tell me anything else?"

Julie had been searching for her sister for a year now. She was not leaving London until she got another lead. She liked Ron, and wanted to trust him, but maintained a distant demeanour.

"Do you think I could come to your place on my way to my hotel?" Julie felt she should do some footwork in her investigation.

"Well, I do have an early morning, but I suppose a night cap would be fine," Ron said as he pressed on his wine glass a little too tightly—his sweaty fingers marking up the deep red stemware.

Ron opened the door of his twelve-year-old Renault to let his passenger in. The door slammed shut as he hurried to his side. Julie studied his hands as he grabbed the clutch and wheel. They drove without saying a word. When they arrived at his walk-up flat, she stood for a moment at the door and took in a deep breath; the smell of fermented cabbage from the second floor corridor, the chipped grey paint in the stairwell, and how nobody was around on a weekend night, all stained her mind.

"This is it. The loo is over there to your left if you want to freshen up."

Julie closed the bathroom door behind her. It was neat and sparse. She opened the medicine cabinet to find a bottle of Paxil and five cotton swabs neatly lying on the aqua-marine glass shelf. The tub was spotless. There was a large container of bleach next to the toilet. After a few moments of exploration, Julie joined Ron on his living room sofa.

"Would you like some more wine or an espresso perhaps?"

"No, that's OK. I won't stay too long. So what did you do together? Where did you go? Did you meet up with anyone else? Did she know anyone else in London?"

"I thought we fancied each other. We went out to eat. We went out for sushi and walks. I showed Valerie around town a bit. We had a nice time. She'll be OK, yes?"

Ron excused himself to the washroom. Julie sat for a few minutes before quietly slipping off her shoes to take a walk around

the flat. She tiptoed straight down the corridor and opened a door. She poked in her head to find a vacuum and a broom. On the left of the utility closet was a bedroom. She listened for Ron in the washroom, and walked towards the made-up, queen-sized bed. She envisioned her sister sleeping on the green sheets and the lumpy, foam-filled pillows. She noticed some blue jeans drying on the radiator grill and a box of tissues on the bedside table. From across the room, Julie noticed a pair of black, sheer stockings on the dresser. Next to the dresser, on the floor, stood a pair of black stiletto shoes. She knew that Valerie never wore stockings, and preferred to wear slacks or pantyhose. Julie picked up the stockings just as she heard the toilet flush, and the hurried flow of the faucet. She dashed back to the living room, and took her place on the sofa.

"Yes, this is only a rental, as I am here temporarily. I'll be leaving for Edinburgh by the spring. I was offered a chair at the university," Ron said as he walked to the basic kitchen to make tea.

"This decor, certainly not my taste. Listen, I hope you find your sister. I'll try to give you any information I can. We can go on a walk-about tomorrow where I'll take you to the places Valerie enjoyed. You can stay here tonight if you like. Julie turned off the lamp and tried to get comfortable under the blanket on the couch.

When she heard Ron snoring from his bedroom, she quietly got up and walked towards his open computer. She looked through his emails for any clues to her sister.

Valerie looked into his favourite pages. There were the predictable pornography sites and a couple of places for automobile lovers. She wondered about the old car.

Just as she was about to walk away from the computer, she heard an instant message come in. Julie went back to the screen.

"Hey there, sexy! What are you wearing for me tonight? Are you wearing the opera gloves?

Julie became curious and played along.

"Yes, I am," Julie said.

"Oh, I love those opera gloves. Run your silky fingers down to your sheer legs, babe."

You wearing the black stockings? The ones with the seams? I am, Baby."

Julie was tired and became very confused. She was certain it was a random message, and went back to the couch. She turned off the light, just to turn it on again and return to the computer.

"Yes, I'm wearing the seamed black stockings. Did you say

you were wearing them, too?" Julie continued.

"Oh, yes. You know I enjoy them. Talk to me, baby. What sexy thing did you do today? Did you see her? What did you find out? Do you think she suspects anything?"

Julie noted the nickname, "Annette4U," as her messages came in and wondered why she expected Ron to be in stockings? Why opera gloves? And what was the interrogation all about? Did she know Ron was to meet her today? The last question didn't sit too well with Julie. She was determined to stay and find out more.

Ron's bedroom door creaked from down the hall. Julie scurried to the kitchen, and fumbled with a glass of water, when Ron walked in.

"Can't sleep?"

"No, ummm, just thirsty."

"I have a sedative if you would like one."

"No, ahh, thank you. I'll just finish my water."

Julie walked back to the couch. She could feel her heart pounding through her chest, ears, and and head. She wanted to bolt out the door, but also wanted to see her private investigation through to the end. She wanted to know about the person on the other side of the computer screen. She had to find out.

Ron walked towards his computer and turned it off. He didn't take the time to read any of the messages. He shuffled back to his bedroom, and closed the door.

Julie lay awake all night. A cold, meat cleaver next to her under the blanket.

SPLITS

by Marian Scott

WE WERE STALLED IN traffic on the Allen Expressway when a young woman jumped out of the red Fiat in front of us. I watched as she ran towards the shoulder, her open bomber jacket billowing in the chilly December wind. She didn't bother fastening it when she stopped to light a cigarette. The Fiat driver pulled the passenger door shut and swung across to the shoulder. Our car inched past him as he sat with his head down and his arms slumped over the steering wheel. I patted Dan's knee.

"Bet they've had a fight."

Dan folded the racing form and looked up to where I was pointing. "Sorry, what'd you say?"

"That couple's had a fight. She must be freezing in that short skirt." We began to pick up speed and glancing in the rearview mirror I noticed the red car tailing the woman.

"What makes you think they've been fightin'?" He didn't wait for my reply. "Subway station's up ahead. Smart lady, she's faster on foot." Glancing at his watch, he added, "Why does everybody haf'ta do their goddamn shoppin' on Sunday?" He turned his attention back to the racing form, traffic picked up, and

as we continued south I thought back to the argument we'd had a few hours ago.

Dan had come down to fix breakfast while I was getting the chili ready for the slow cooker. He poured himself a coffee and offered to cut up the onions. I told him I didn't want his help, and ran the cold water to dissipate the fumes. I began dicing the celery, and finally asked him what I'd been waiting to ask him since yesterday.

"How'd you feel about coming with me to the cemetery later? It's getting late in the season, and we still haven't laid down the Christmas wreath."

He remained expressionless and didn't reply for a minute or two. "I'll go on one condition. You drop me off afterwards at P.M.s. Big Jake's runnin' in the ninth down at Sarasota." Next thing I knew the paring knife had slipped, my finger was bleeding, and expletives were flying out of my mouth. I ran my hand under cold water until the bright red stream stopped, and ignoring the towel he offered me, I reached inside the cupboard for a bandage.

"I thought you agreed no more sports bars." Turning to face him I said, "You're burning money faster than I can make it. Christmas is only three weeks away." He put on his reading glasses, pulled the racing form out of his back pocket, and without looking up he walked out of the kitchen.

On the way to Pine Hills he had said, "Why don't you just mail in a cheque to cover the cost of maintainin' your parents' graves? Nobody else in your family can be bothered with this groundskeepin' shit ... uh-uh. 'Leave it to Marie,' they say, 'she's better at that kinda thing.'"

The argument didn't stop there. As soon as we entered the main gates of the cemetery I pulled over and parked. "Actually, Dan, forget about ever coming here with me again. If we're being totally honest, why *did* you come? You never wanted to visit my parents when they were alive. You only phoned them when you wanted to borrow money."

"Whoaa," he interrupted. "First you drag me out here, and then you start with the bullshit." Tapping his forefinger on the dashboard he said, "I don't need any of this." I started the engine, drove close to the gravesite, and parked. When I went to open the trunk, Dan was there beside me, reaching in and taking the wreath out of its plastic wrap. We walked over to the grave, and I stood and watched as he jammed the metal rods into the frozen ground. He

turned to ask me if it looked okay, and wiping a tear off my cheek, I asked him to move the wreath over slightly so the inscription on the headstone could be seen. He shoved his hands in his pocket, then asked for the car keys. I handed them over and said I needed a minute. The car horn blasted as I finished saying a prayer. I quickly read the inscription: *Always Together* Helen Kowalczuk April 23, 1940 – November 19, 2006 Beloved Wife of Walter Kowalczuk, December 4, 1937 – January 21, 2007.

Dan came home around 9:30. He hung up his jacket and walked into the kitchen rubbing his hands together. "Chili smells good." He opened the fridge and grabbed a beer. "Wish you could'a seen Big Jake pull out'ta the back stretch, 19-1 odds." He leaned over, kissed my cheek. "I got the tri."

"Just get a bowl for yourself, I've already eaten." I crossed my arms, and leaning back on the counter I was tempted to ask him if he'd blown it all paying back his buddies. Instead I said, "Listen, before you sit down, I want to say something. There's stuff we need to work on." Dan grabbed the salt shaker and avoided my stare. "You've got it in your head my family thinks they're better than you but it shouldn't matter. Mom adored you, and Dad loved you too, in his own way."

"Okay, that's enough," he said heading over to the table. "You haven't asked me about the win." I sat down across from him, my chin resting in my hands, and I asked him how much.

"Enough to take you out someplace really nice for dinner. See what happens when the horsies call and I hit it on the nose?"

"Go ahead, have fun. Next time, you talk to the creditors on the phone. I've run out of excuses."

"You didn't let me finish, Marie. I said I caught the triactor." He put down his spoon, reached into his pocket and pulled out a wad of bills. "It paid over two thou."

"Wow." I stared at the money, wondered what he'd say if I suggested we pay some bills instead of going out for dinner. I held out my hand without saying anything and he reached over and put the bundle in my hand.

"Do what you want with it."

"I'll go to the bank first thing tomorrow then." I waited for his response, but he pushed his chair away from the table and asked if I wanted a beer.

"No thanks, I had a glass of red earlier." He got another beer for himself and sat back down. I looked across at him and cocked

my head to one side. "That couple fighting on the Allen today, they reminded me of us and that huge fight we had before we got married." He didn't say anything, just gave me a blank look. "I can still picture the whole thing like it was yesterday. We were on Dundas on our way to meet Mark and Colleen at Doc's Place. You were going to ask Mark to be your best man ... we were walking along and you said maybe we should postpone the wedding. I threw my engagement ring at you and took off. You caught up with me, took my hand, and put the ring back on my finger."

"Yeah, now I remember." Rubbing his stomach, Dan belched loudly. "Didn't you tell me later Mark and Colleen saw the whole fight or something?"

"That's right. They were on the streetcar passing us as I was throwing my ring at you. Coll phoned me up the next day to ask me about it. She said Mark had got cold feet before their wedding, too. You know, it's too bad they're not together anymore. They seemed to be in for the long haul." I stood up and unplugged the slow cooker. "When's the last time you heard from Mark?"

"Been a couple of years now." Dan followed me to the living room, and we sat down on the couch. "Boy, me and him had some fun times tendin' bar together. Did I ever tell you about our first gig?" I nodded and plumped up a pillow behind me. "Those were crazy times. Right out of bartendin' school, and they throw us into the lunch crowd at Lord Stanley's. We get there about fifteen minutes before the action starts," Dan stretched his legs and rested the beer bottle on his thigh. "Neither of us knows where any of the supplies are kept, the orders start comin' in, people lined up all along the counter. The regular bartender was off, and the rest of the staff knew shit all."

"What a pressure cooker."

"You're tellin' me. Anyway, this guy orders a gin and soda. So I pour the soda into the gin only to have it sent back. They forgot to tell us at school about splits – that's what they call the bottles of soda or ginger ale, they're about the size of ... say those little juice bottles in the fridge. The split should've been served separately so the customer can pour it himself." Scratching his head he said, "Geez, I can't remember now if I quit or they fired me." He put his arm around me. "Mark, he did okay. Far's I know he's still tendin' bar."

"You should call him up and see if he wants to come over sometime for dinner. He must be lonely living on his own."

"Nah, it's kinda awkward. The last time we had a few drinks all he could talk about was Colleen and how she wouldn't even let him talk to the kids over the phone." He gulped the last of his beer.

"Did you ever find out what caused the break-up? You and Mark were closer than me and Coll. I think she got hurt about something I said or did. She seemed kinda fragile. Of course, after they started having kids, we didn't have much in common."

"Guys don't go pourin' out their guts the way you women do, 'cept after a few beers. But he never said anythin' to me."

"What worries me is how one day things might totally fall apart between us — look at earlier today. Do you think it's the same in other relationships? Maybe anger builds and builds like a slow burn, or one day everything blows up, and that's the end?"

"You gotta stop readin' those women's magazines, for chrissake." He rubbed the top of my head, adding, "Too much Oprah." I gave him a soft punch in the arm, and he bent over, clutching it in mock pain. "But seriously, some couples get lucky, Marie, and who knows why things work out for Couple A but not for Couple B. Look at your parents. They were together for what, fifty years? Anyway you look at it, it's a crap shoot."

"Thanks, I feel so much better."

"Hey, do you think we could get together tonight, if you know what I mean?" He gave me a wink and turned his head towards the stairs.

"I'll think about it." I caught the look of disappointment on his face and said, "Okay, okay, but I want to catch the news first." He started heading up the stairs, and I turned on City Pulse. I recognized the red car immediately. "Dan," I yelled, "hurry, come here." He ran into the living room and sat down beside me. The accident had occurred at Eglinton and the Allen around 4:30 p.m.

"Hold on," said Dan, "I can't believe it, that's Mark being interviewed." Mark, sitting inside the Fiat, ashen-faced, said that it had all happened in a split second. The blue van skidded on a patch of ice and struck his girlfriend as she was crossing the road.

"She was on her cell." Mark's voice faltered as he looked away from the camera. "My guess is she didn't even see what hit her." The reporter concluded by saying the woman's condition was unknown at this time. I looked over at Dan and touched his arm.

SHOELESS IN BEVERLY HILLS
by Reva Stern

AFTER FOUR YEARS OF self-imposed celibacy following a soul-numbing divorce, my friend Carole was insisting that I leave Toronto and the chilly vestiges of my former relationship and visit Los Angeles for a while in search of Mr. Soul Mate.

I had directed Carole in three critically acclaimed plays, and she had been most generous in her appreciation. Her invitation to join her at a Beverly Hills dinner party was followed by her plea that she was "simply desperate" to have me meet the wealthy hosts. Her fervid hope was that they would invest handsomely in a perfect little off-Broadway musical she was passionate about. My secret hope was that I might meet a handsome guy that I could be perfectly passionate about.

In Carole's estimation, this dinner could turn out to be a *coup de grâce* (or was it *foie gras*?): They would finance the show, I would direct it, and she, of course, would star in it.

I left Toronto on a cold November morning and arrived on the same morning in the land of sun, sand, and silicone.

Just days before the big dinner, Carole gave me a crash course in the behavioural antics of a Beverly Hills hostess.

"The only thing you need to know about these zillionaires" she warned "is that: (*a*) they are wild about Canadians 'cause you're all so polite, (*b*) they are clean freaks, and (*c*) they eat only organic food."

So, having been forewarned, I chose my "coming to dinner gift" with great care. I put together a gift basket filled with all kinds of noble treats like herbal teas, organic chocolate, and plant-unscented soaps and body oils. I wrapped it all in recyclable paper and tied it with raw natural raffia.

No one really dresses for dinner in L.A. but, since *I am Canadian,* I wanted to set a higher standard. I wore a little black designer outfit and my new, exorbitantly priced, Donald Pliner spike-heeled boots.

My taxi pulled up in front of the majestic Spanish Villa at precisely 7:39 pm. Carole was due to arrive at 7:40 pm. Dinner was called for 7:30 pm.

"Never arrive exactly on time or, even worse, ... early, unless you're wearing polyester and a pocket protector," she had cynically warned.

As I hoisted the gift basket onto my hip, I watched a hairy little hound run through a flowerbed, scamper onto the landing, and then curl up on the welcome mat, where he began to explore his nether regions with furious gusto.

I wasn't sure what the protocol was in such a situation. Do you throw a bucket of cold water on the critter so he'll do it in private next time? Or, do you simply ignore his earnest exploration like you do a toddler who just discovered the southern-most regions of his body?

Just as I was steering my stilettos onto the landing, the frenzied hound made a beeline past me down the stairs, in pursuit of a lovely looking white poodle attached to a bejewelled leash held by an iPod-wearing-uniformed nanny.

The majestic door opened and there stood my Hollywood hostess. There was no mistaking her. Not that she was a celebrity. She was actually more of a scientific project: bottle blonde with plastic breasts, chemical lips, and a biological forehead.

"Hi, do come in. Carole should be here any minute... she's always irritatingly late. I'm so thrilled you could come... and thank you for the lovely basket," she purred as I handed it over and stepped inside.

"Can I ask you please to remove your shoes?" She chanted.

I blinked.

Many uncomfortable seconds passed.

"You want me to take off my boots?" I choked back a strangling gasp.

"Yes, if you don't mind."

I detected a definite threatening overtone.

"Uh, no... of course not." I said, remembering to be a polite Canadian. "I've never been asked to do that before. Is there a reason why you would ask me, in particular?" I enquired, wondering if there was some ugly rumour in the wind concerning my feet.

"Oh, heavens no, it's not just you, dear. See, there are already six pairs of visitors' footwear accounted for," she proudly proclaimed as she opened the closet door with a flourish. "We ask all our guests to remove their shoes so they won't bring germs into our home. We're crazed to avoid bacteria. We're very health conscious here in California... but, of course, coming from such a frigid climate, you wouldn't have to worry about diseases the way we do in this hot hemisphere."

I sucked back a weary sigh, wanting desperately to explain that I didn't live in the cryogenic reaches of the North West Territories or that looking at my unpedicured feet might bring on a greater case of the runs for her guests than anything that might have piggy-backed onto the sole of my boot. But, just as I was about to take a stab at exemption, our mutual friend arrived.

After the air kissing was done, the hostess cheerily asked Carole to remove her shoes.

"Honey, these are $450.00 Manola Blaniks. I'd rather take off my bra and panties!"

"That won't be necessary," the hostess quipped, "Just the Blaniks, please!"

Neither Carole nor I had made a move to complete the task that was asked of us before a flurry at the door drew our attention. Suddenly the same frisky dog I had seen minutes earlier was jumping all over the lady of the house, who was being coaxed to her well waxed knees by the wily little hound. The sight of that canine tongue licking every inch of our hostess's taut face brought a chuckle to my heart... but once the exuberant pup began slurping at her Revlon candy-pink lips, it was more than I could bear.

"Catherine, sorry, but do you realize where that dog's tongue has been?" I sputtered.

"I assure you," she confidently replied "Benito's tongue is a

darn sight cleaner than your boots."

With that, I quietly removed my spiffy, vein-popping, new footwear while Carole sashayed into the powder room, presumably to cool off.

As I followed the hostess into the elegant parlour, I was certain that my fabulous designer outfit was being undermined by my gnarly bunioned feet.

I was expecting to meet the owners of the other six pairs of relinquished shoes, but was not prepared to meet a seventh. He was a six-foot, Cole Haan-loafer-wearing Adonis.

"Michael, this is Carole's friend... uh... ... uh could you introduce her to everyone while I check on our dinner?"

I rather enjoyed watching our germaphobic hostess stammering over my name, which she thought she'd forgotten but had actually never known.

Adonis smiled comfortably as my blush level rose to crimson.

"Hi, I'm Michael Silver, and you are?"

"Uh... oh, hi, Michael... I'm Rachel Gold. Before we join the others, could I ask you a rather forward question?"

"Well, Rachel, since Gold trumps Silver you get to ask me any question you like."

"Okay. How come you get to keep your shoes on?"

"That's it? That's the best you can do? You're easy."

"You see, Catherine's husband also likes to keep his shoes on, and, and, since I'm his podiatrist, we both benefit from my clever advice to keep those arch supports under foot at all times."

As we took our seats at the great dining table, Michael graciously introduced me to the six other barefoot guests that included: a heart surgeon, a tax lawyer, and a screenwriter who all seemed equally intent on keeping the tongue-happy-hound with an obvious foot fetish away from their vulnerable toes.

I, on the other hand, barely noticed Benito slurping voraciously at my curling toes as Michael set off fireworks in my head.

Carole's score for the evening was... one win: she kept her Manola Blaniks on through the entire evening. One loss: Catherine declined to finance her show.

As for me, Benito chewed the toes out of my budget-busting Pliner boots, I broke out in hives from doggy dander, and then topped the evening off with an anaphylactic reaction from the hazelnuts the

chef was inspired to put into the crème brulée as a taste surprise.

Since Michael's car was the only one not trapped in driveway gridlock, he was elected to drive me to the hospital. He stayed around until the welts receded and I could breathe on my own; then he left and I haven't heard from him since.

That same night, Carole brought the shoeless heart surgeon (also known as chief of staff at the hospital) along to assure prompt attention for me. He stayed long after Carole and the podiatrist had left the building.

Dr. Warren Crystal and I have been seeing each other for eight months now.

On Valentine's Day he bought me a pair of Donald Pliner boots that were identical to the one's that Mussolini (or whatever the hound's name was) had for dinner that fateful evening. I'm beginning to believe that my heart surgeon just might be my Dr. Soul Mate.

As for the hostess, we heard that two weeks after "the event," she went to a health spa for a much-needed rest and ended up with a horrendous toenail fungus. People really should keep their shoes on, don't you think?

MY GRANDFATHER CLOCK
by Sandor Stern

MANY YEARS AGO, WHILE on a Sunday drive in the country with my wife, we stumbled upon an auction of contents from the home of a recently deceased farmer. The items on display were functional, plain, and inexpensive. We made a perfunctory pass through the house and were about to leave when I spotted an old grandfather clock that drew my attention. It stood dusty and silent in a corner of the living room, its hands pointing out the wrong time, its tarnished pendulum motionless, its weights resting on the cabinet bottom. Its wood frame was dark mahogany, unadorned with filigree or scrollwork. A small section of veneer had somehow been ripped away, leaving an unsightly scar. Its face was an aged cream colour with a circle of Roman numerals marking off the time.

Closer examination revealed a tiny lever on the face that allowed one to switch among three different chimes: Winchester, Westminster, and Windsor. I asked the auctioneer whether the clock functioned, but he had no idea. Curious to see what price would be paid by the professional hunters usually found at these auctions, I convinced my wife to stay awhile.

The auction began with few participants. Items were

selling for embarrassingly low prices, and it became apparent that professional hunters had bypassed this auction. When the clock came up for bidding, no one expressed an interest. I bought that clock for eighty dollars. For another twenty dollars, a farmer with a pickup truck delivered it to my house. A repairman cleaned the mechanism and replaced the missing veneer. The clock functioned perfectly. More than that, it chimed every quarter hour in whatever mode I chose. I loved that clock.

Over the next twelve years, the clock travelled with us across the continent from Toronto to Los Angeles. And, no matter the decor of any new home, that clock found its place. But then, my wife and I divorced. The clock stayed with her. I didn't ask for it. I didn't want it. As much as I missed it, it represented a life and relationship that was no longer mine.

Five years after that divorce, I married again. On my wedding day, a gift from my parents was delivered to my house. It was a grandfather clock. They knew how much I had loved my old clock and wanted to rekindle that feeling in me. It was a newly crafted antique replica of polished pinewood with embossed scrollwork. The brass pendulum and winding weights gleamed. The pristine face featured delicate hands and an emblem of a globe across which were written the words *Tempus fugit*. It had a Westminster chime that lengthened from the quarter hour through the hour so that there was no mistake what quarter hour you were hearing.

Beautiful as it was, the clock rekindled nothing in me. Being newly crafted, it had no character and no history. My parents were not sophisticated people. The concept of old or antique was foreign to them. "New" was good. And they had spent a considerable sum on this clock. It would have hurt them terribly to know I did not share their enthusiasm. Returning it was not an option. So I thanked them and placed the clock in my house and learned to live with it. In the back of my mind was the idea that some day in the future I would devise a way to replace it without hurting their feelings.

Two years after my marriage, my father died of a sudden heart attack. The family rallied around my mother who had lost her partner of fifty years. My brother and I brought her from Toronto to live in Los Angeles where she could be close to us. All thoughts of that grandfather clock vanished in the years that followed. My wife and I purchased a new home where the clock found a place in the little used formal dining room, somewhat out of place next to the antique furnishings. But there was no way that I could bring myself

to get rid of it, not with my mother living so close by.

After a few years in Los Angeles, my mother longed to return to Toronto and the company of my sisters and aunts. I knew the day we flew her back that she would never return to Los Angeles. Her health was failing and travel was no longer easy for her. Just before midnight, in April of 1994, my mother died. I had just returned home from my brother's wedding when the phone call came. I made arrangements for my wife and me to fly to Toronto the following morning.

That night, sleep was impossible. Giving up the futile attempt, I got out of bed and went downstairs. As I approached the kitchen, I heard the chime of the grandfather clock and felt drawn towards it. It stood silent in the dining room, its hands pointing out the time of 3:45. For no apparent reason, I sat in a chair and gazed upon it. Immediately, a flood of memories washed over me, each revealing my parents' joyful faces through all the days and months and years of our lives together. In the midst of those memories, the clock chimed again. A quarter hour had passed in an instant. But something more than time had changed. In that lyrical chime I distinctly heard the sweet voice of my mother; and, as the clock struck four, the deep resonant voice of my father rang out. Tears of shame welled up in me. Dear God. All those years I had seen only a clock. They had given me a gift of love.

Years have passed since that revelation. In my home, the clock continues to chime the quarters and strike the hours. And moments occur when the buzz of daily existence fails to drown out the sound. Then I distinctly hear the voices of my parents, and I thank God that the present they gave me thirty years ago has become their presence in my heart in this moment.

WELCOME TO TORONTO
by Steven Hilliard Stern

I ARRIVED BY COLONIAL Coach at the midtown terminal in
Toronto on a hot, muggy day in July 1954 — the same year Bill Haley
and the Comets introduced "Rock Around the Clock" on the sound
track of *Black Board Jungle*, a seminal event in any seventeen-year-
old boy's life.

As I exited the bus I noticed my suitcase sitting on the curb.
The bus driver continued to pull luggage from the belly of the bus.
Passengers milled around waiting for their bags. I reached
for my suitcase.

"Hey, is that yours?" someone shouted.

I turned to look. The bus driver was eyeing me.

"Yeah… it's mine," I said.

"You sure?"

I was sure, but his attitude made me feel insecure so I picked
the suitcase up to my face and took a good look.

"Yeah. It's mine."

"You only got the one?"

Why was he picking on me? What did I do?

"I only have this one," I said, now thoroughly embarrassed.

"Okay," he said without looking back, continuing to pull bags from the bus.

Did he think I would steal somebody else's suitcase? Why would I do that? How would I know if some other guy's clothes would fit me? They could be too small or too big, or worse... ugly. Maybe he thinks I'm really poor because I have only one bag. To hell with him. Someday I'll be a big movie star and he'll still be a bus driver. That will be my revenge.

Nearly every summer since my brother and I were about twelve and eleven my parents sent us to Toronto for a week's vacation. We stayed at our Bubbie's house; she was my father's mother. I was headed for Bubbie's, but this time it was different. I was about to start my first year in Film and Television Arts at The Ryerson Institute of Technology. My brother had already completed his first year in Medical School at the University of Toronto.

As I wandered the busy streets, I quickly forgot about the incident with the bus driver. Here I was, a young man from the small town of Prescott, Ontario; I was in Toronto... electric streetcars clanging along the rails that confined them to the middle of every main street. There were automobiles whizzing along, crisscrossing behind and in front of them... brakes slamming, horns blowing, people yelling and pushing towards the streetcars as they came to a stop. The folding doors opened and people poured into the street as others pushed and shoved their way on board. I almost lost my suitcase in the melee while trying to climb the steps into the streetcar.

The Bay Street line, then a transfer to the College Street line, which stopped at Bathurst Street, a two block walk, and I was on Palmerston Avenue, my destination. In approximately twenty minutes I'd gone from Chinatown to Jewish town.

I fell in love with Toronto from my first summer visit. The city reminded me of the ones I saw in the movies every Saturday afternoon at the only theatre in Prescott. Toronto had a movie theatre on every block... or so it seemed. There were tons of restaurants, clothing stores, department stores. There was Sunnyside Beach on Lake Ontario, with a pool larger than an Olympic size; and Sunnyside had an amusement park with the largest Ferris wheel and rollercoaster I had ever seen... even in the movies.

And the aromas! The delis and the bakeries! It made me salivate just to walk down Spadina Avenue.

There were so many things to do and so little time. But not

this time. Now I was here for good—or at least until I could get to Hollywood.

As I walked down Palmerston Avenue I could see Bubbie's house. Even from half a block away I could see she had given the front porch a summer coat of paint. It was a ritual. Colour did not matter. This year it was bright red.

I opened the front door, stepped into the vestibule, and shouted, "Bubbie, you here?" Before I reached the kitchen, I heard, "Hillel, is dat you?"

As I entered the kitchen, she was already crying with joy, her arms outstretched to give me a hug and a kiss. She was the only person who ever showed me that kind of affection. And, although I was uncomfortable with it, I loved it. When she finally let go, she reached inside her sleeve for the ever present Kleenex to dab her eyes. "So, ven did you get in?"

"Just now, as you were getting up from the table. You didn't notice?"

She looked confused, so I offered a big smile. She gets the joke.

"Oy, Hillel, alvays joking mit me." She laughed.

"So Bubbie, where's my brother?"

"Oy! I tol' a'im he shute meet you at da bus but he says you no da vay. Anyway, he's mit his friends on the next street over."

"Okay, I'm gonna go find him."

"Bring him back mit you. I'll make a nice dinner."

I walked over to the next block and started down the street towards a group of young guys. It was too far away to determine if my brother was in the group. A few more steps and I saw a guy turn around and head towards me. He started to run. It was my brother! I couldn't believe it! He was running towards me. He was happy to see me. He was actually excited to see me. Mom and dad should have seen this... they would not have believed it. I saw it and could not believe it. He was running. I stopped. I had a big smile on my face. "Oh Lord, I thought. "I hope he is not going to lay one of those big 'Bubbie' hugs on me... not here in the middle of the street."

My brother was gasping for breath. He was sweating profusely, but, before I was able to utter a word, he quietly blurted out... with menacing conviction, "If you call me 'Stinky' in front of my friends, I'll kill you."

Welcome to Toronto. We were definitely not in Prescott any more. This was surely a new world. No more 'Stinky.'

Why would he think that I would call him 'Stinky' in front of his friends? I asked myself. Then I answered myself… because I *would* have called him 'Stinky' in front of his friends. Not out of malice but out of habit. I had forgotten why we called him Stinky Stern over the years, and who had stuck him with this ridiculous, disgusting nickname, but everybody in Prescott called him Stinky. Even when he graduated from Prescott High School as the valedictorian of his class, Mr. Cousins, the strict, conservative principal, introduced him with, "…and it is with great pride I introduce to you this year's valedictorian, Sandor 'Stinky' Stern." It got a good laugh, and, to his credit, my brother did not flinch.

But it was coming back to me now — the guy who had started the nickname. He was a nice guy. A little strange, some would say. Different maybe. He often wore white buck loafers and a maroon blazer with white ribbing on the lapel, and a crest on the pocket. If it sounded like something out of a Gene Kelly movie, you would be right. The big difference here was that the shoes were not really white bucks — they were an old pair of brown shoes painted white. And the jacket was really a smoking jacket with a patch on the pocket. He wasn't exactly Gene Kelly, but he was obviously a guy who tap danced to the beat of a different tune.

Anyway, I confess, it was me. I gave him the nickname. I even remember the incident.

Growing up, my brother and I would get into fistfights. He would knock me down, beat me up, but I would always get up again. I would wear him out. He would plead with me to stop fighting, but I would just keep coming.

On one such occasion, while we were locked in mortal combat, our mother called us for dinner. My brother was hungry and wanted to go in, but I wouldn't let him. I wanted to keep fighting. When he tried going in, I'd yell, "Run, you chicken, run." Finally, he just gave up and went inside, leaving me out there alone, crying.

A few moments went by and he stuck his head out the door. "Mom says you better come in for dinner right now or she's calling Dad."

Dad — The Enforcer. That got my attention. I moved towards the house. Frustrated, searching for something profound, something devastating to say, and then it came to me: "You know what?"

"What?"

"You stink, that's what."

"Yeah, so do you."

"Yeah, but you stink more and that's what I'm gonna call you from now on: Stinky Stern. And I'm gonna tell everybody that's your real name."

"Shut up."

"Yeah, well… I'm gonna tell Dad you told me to shut up."

I was stunned back to the present by the sound of my brother's voice, "Did you hear me? I'll kill you!"

"What? Yeah, okay, what should I call you?"

"Sandy."

"You're not 'Sandy' your name is 'Sandor.'"

"That's what my friends here call me."

"I'm not gonna call you 'Sandy.'"

"Okay, fine. Call me 'Sandor.'"

"Well, maybe if I get used to it, I'll call you 'Sandy.'"

My big brother smiled. "Fine. Let's go and meet the guys."

As we started towards his friends, I relayed Bubbie's message about dinner.

"You want to do that?" he asked.

"Yeah. Why not? I like her cooking."

"Wait 'til you've eaten it for a year. Let me tell you about her green potato pancakes."

MARRIED LIFE
by *Anna Stitski*

"IT FEELS GOOD TO be home," Laura thought as she walked up the winding staircase to her bedroom. Rufus, her apricot poodle, trotted along behind her. She dropped her suitcase on the floor, turned on the bedroom stereo and plopped herself on the neatly made bed. She thought about her husband Bob and all the things she loved about him - he was thoughtful, organized and so romantic. Her friends were always complaining about their husbands who were slobs, but not Laura. Bob was neat and tidy and always cleaned up.

Laura looked around the room. They had just redecorated and she loved all the changes: burgundy walls, beige ultra suede bedding, and animal print accent pillows and window treatments. And there... what was that sticking out of the bottom of the closet door?

Laura jumped off the bed and opened the closet door. "That bastard!" she thought. "How dare he? I go away for a few days and come home to find this!" She looked at the stuff carelessly thrown on the closet floor: black lace bra and matching panties, garter-belt, fishnet stockings, lipstick and perfume. None of this belonged to her. And his usually crisp white Armani shirt, lay crumpled and

lipstick-stained.

"Is he a complete idiot? Did he think he could get away with this?" she asked Rufus, who blankly looked up at her. "He promised me it had ended. Told the counsellor he got it out of his system. I thought I could trust him again... liar!" She burst into tears. Laura heard his car drive up and quickly wiped her tears. She sat on the edge of the bed. How was she going to handle this? She stared at her wedding photo hanging on the wall.

"Hi Hon," said Bob, pushing the front door open. "I missed you. I brought take-out from your favourite restaurant. Thought we could have a quiet, candle-lit dinner." The house was quiet. That's strange he thought, as he mindlessly changed his shoes. Her car is in the driveway. "Laura, are you home?" Maybe she took Rufus for a walk. But just then, Rufus came bounding down the stairs.

"Come on pup, I'll let you out." He headed to the back door through the kitchen, putting the take-out on the table along the way. Maybe she's having a bubble bath, he thought as he opened the door and let the dog out. He knew she liked to unwind in a tub full of bubbles after her business trips.

Bob walked to the bottom of the stairs and hollered, "Laura, are you up there?" No answer but he could hear music coming from the bedroom. He walked back to the kitchen, let the dog in and glanced at the wine bottles in the rack. He was glad he replenished the supply before Laura got back. She'd never know her favourite bottle of red was consumed while she was away. He found its replacement and opened it. Nothing better than a nice glass of wine while soaking in the tub, he thought as he poured two glasses. "Maybe she would like a bit of company," he commented to Rufus. When they renovated the ensuite, they had an extra large tub installed, a tub that easily accommodated two.

He found candles and matches in a drawer. Bob shuddered; did he remember to clean up? Well of course he did. He always cleaned up. He was always extra careful. Candlelight, wine and bubbles. Bob liked a little romance before dinner. He put the glasses, candles and wine on a tray and started up the stairs. "Laura, I'm home," he called. Still no answer. What if she fell asleep in the tub and drowned... Oh my God! "Laura!" he yelled, racing up the stairs, two at a time. Rufus was right behind him. He kicked the bedroom door open and found Laura sitting on the edge of the bed, holding the black lace bra in her right hand. "Uh oh," he thought as he dropped the tray.

"What's this?" Laura asked, looking him straight in the eye. "And this isn't my brand of perfume," she said, holding up the bottle of Escape with her left hand. "You know I can't wear this; it gives me a headache." She flung the bra at him. This startled Rufus, who ran under the bed. "It's not mine. I've never been an A-cup!"

What could he say? His mind was racing. The lipstick bounced off his head. "Not my colour," she said. "What other surprises will I find? I go away for two days and you lose control. How could you?"

"How could I? It... was part of a gift for you. But you had to go snooping and ruin the surprise."

"Surprise gift? Bullshit! Last surprise gift you bought me was the satellite dish. And I wasn't snooping. You were careless and left your 'gift' lying around. Besides, hooker red lipstick is not my colour!"

"Okay. I'm sorry. I made a mistake. I'm weak. I promise it won't happen again. I'll start seeing the counsellor again. Please, forgive me."

"I can't live like this. We've been through this before and I can't go through this again. It's obvious you have no control. Just pack your things and get out."

"But Laura, please. I love you. I need your help. Besides, I have no place to go," he pleaded.

"How about home to mummy? Her clothes may be more flattering to your figure. I don't really care where you go Bob. Just get out. I'm tired of you ruining my designer dresses."

"But I've always replaced them."

"You're not getting it Bob. I can't take it anymore. I'm just sick and tired of finding you in my clothes. Just pack your bags and get out. I need time to think." Laura looked down at his feet, "And one more thing, take off my shoes before you leave."

PROFESSOR Z. W. SHEN
by Hailun Tang

IT WAS 1968. THE shocking news spread rapidly through the entire institute. "Professor Shen was detained last night by the Red Guards!"

But why?

The Chinese Cultural Revolution began in August of 1966 and lasted for ten years. In that decade, the entire country was turned upside down. What had been good became bad: traditions, schools, and research. And, anything associated with Western culture was banned.

Professor Z. W. Shen was a senior researcher at an institute in Shanghai, and a professor at the university affiliated with the institute. Because of his renowned scholarship, he was named the chief editor of the institute's magazine, which was published in both Chinese and English. I was a student at the university. He taught courses in inorganic chemistry, biochemistry and metabolism. After I graduated in 1964, I took graduate studies at the institute where he worked.

I can still picture him vividly: tall, slim, and bald. He liked to walk up the four floors to his office with a book or a magazine tucked

armpit of his navy blue jacket. But the short walk often turned into a long march because he, a popular professor, would constantly be stopped by students asking questions. He would first listen with narrowed, smiling eyes, which peered at us through his thick lenses, and then answer in his soft bass voice.

He entranced us with his lectures, which he presented with high spirit and humour. He had a knack for turning the most complicated concepts into fascinating stories, which were easier for us to digest. Often times, being so thoroughly absorbed by his lectures I would realize I hadn't taken a single note, a disaster we called "flying."

It was easy to pass his exams by answering the general questions. But to get an "A", we had to intelligently answer one particular question, a "live" one. This question was never from a textbook—something that would really make us think, and never easy! I remember one clearly: "How many water-exits are there in our bodies?" After this exam, we all nervously compared our answers but only found that we'd missed all kinds of exits. Some forgot tears, some forgot saliva, and I forgot my foot sweat. Great!

Soon after Professor Shen's lock-up, the Red Guards announced that he was accused of being a foreign spy because he had studied in Canada and the United States. I learned from another professor who had shared his cell during the lock-up, that Professor Shen suffered tremendously. The Red Guards beat him cruelly because he refused to falsely confess to any spying, or to wrongly accuse any of his friends or students of doing anti-revolutionary work. Some others had made such accusations in order to protect themselves.

I still remember a Red Guard, red faced, dash out of the "jail," shouting to us, "Shen held the paper so close to his thick lenses that it touched his nose and slowly wrote, word by word, a confession of innocence!" Having heard how Professor Shen had teased that Red Guard by exaggerating his poor vision, I worried about him. Red Guards should not be teased. However, I really admired his courage and his unflagging humour even during his miserable time. What a fighter!

Professor Shen was finally released after six months detainment when they couldn't prove his guilt. He had by then earned a new name—"Shen Lao," a name later recognized within the scientific community all over China. The honorific "Lao" denoted a senior scholar, not only of great fame, but also deserving of great

respect and love from all of his students and colleagues.

In 1975, the political situation loosened up somewhat. We were again able to talk about scientific research. One day, my colleague ZhiAn sat down with me to discuss how to catch up with the rest of the world. We both realized the importance of English for us to keep abreast of progress and discoveries in science and technology, most of which were published in Western magazines, in English.

"How will you study English?" ZhiAn asked.

"I'm thinking about asking Shen Lao to teach me English in private," I said, "but…" I froze. *Why would he, a target of the revolution and a suspected foreign agent, risk his life to teach me, a nobody, English?* My heart sank. But my urge to learn persisted. *Why not ask?* I thought. After a few days of self-debate, I went to see him and timidly, I made my request.

With a gleam in his eye he smiled and nodded without hesitation. He would teach ZhiAn and me English! I was overjoyed by how easily and simply I'd recruited the best teacher. I ran at once to tell ZhiAn the good news. Overwhelmed, I promised myself to study hard to repay his kindness.

Our group of three began our English classes in 1975. To avoid new political troubles for Shen Lao, we needed a secure place. ZhiAn and I searched the entire campus and spotted a small box-like concrete cabin buried within a stand of huge trees. Ah, "the Coffin!" In the early years of the Cultural Revolution it had been used to hold a famous political target, but now totally deserted. We pried open the door and at once choked on the damp air and the rotten smell. No wonder people called it "the Coffin." The only window was so tiny that not much sunlight could penetrate, and a single bulb hung down from the ceiling into the middle of the room.

A few stools lay on the cement floor. We pulled them up and dusted them. Although there was neither heat in the winter nor air-conditioning in the summer, we didn't care. We had found a secret classroom for learning a forbidden language!

Every Friday from 4 p.m. to 5 p.m. was our Happy English Hour, for learning English. In the first cold winter when the temperature was below zero, the three of us huddled together, knee to knee, to stay warm, while Shen Lao charmed us with stories in English. His jokes made us laugh and kept us warm. We were completely absorbed in his English world, forgetting our freezing toes. Then came the hot summer, and he had us write stories in English.

"Write, write and write some more. That makes you think in English. An exercise you must practise," he said. But I didn't have much free time for English writing. My research put a demand on all of my time. *What to do?* I was troubled. Miraculously, I found myself beginning to create English stories unconsciously during my morning dreams before waking up. It felt as if I was sitting in front of Shen Lao's kind face, composing English, sentence by sentence, and then reading to him, silently. It was exactly what I did in high school to solve difficult math problems, and amazingly it worked again to write English stories.

That summer, it didn't matter that the temperature soared above 37 degrees Celsius. We still locked ourselves inside "the Coffin" to read our assignments, aloud, and Shen Lao would correct us. We enjoyed the class so much that we didn't notice our shirts soaked with sweat. We were lost in the English world, but this time, it was ours!

Shen Lao was a patient teacher. Never once was he unhappy with our not-good-enough homework or disappointed in us when we didn't understand him. "If you don't understand, that's my fault," he said, and he'd explain his lesson again from a different angle until we understood. He wanted us to read a wide range of English, not only science papers but also literature. "Read, read, and read again. Only then will you learn and improve your English."

I follow this advice faithfully even today. I laugh when I recall how difficult it was to read my first English novel, *The Count of Monte Cristo*. I can still feel my embarrassment. I opened the novel and started to read keenly. The very first sentence had two dozen words, more than half of which were new to me. So I consulted my Chinese-English Dictionary and was immediately bewildered. *How am I going to figure out which definition will fit the sentence when some words have multiple meanings and some aren't even listed?*

"Guess if you can." Shen Lao had encouraged me.

So that's what I did. I continued reading, writing, and guessing. Soon I began to really enjoy reading English novels for entertainment, not merely for learning the language. Marvellously, the three of us continued the Happy English Hour for a year and a half. By then, I had discovered with great joy that my vocabulary had expanded, my comprehension had escalated, and my reading and listening skills had leaped forward. What an encouraging achievement!

But not long after, the political wind changed its direction,

and the entire country was tightened again. One Friday afternoon when Shen Lao was regaling us with some funny slang, I heard faint footsteps and then saw a Red Guard peek through the window. He left quickly, but my heart almost jumped out of my chest. "A Red Guard!" I whispered to Shen Lao and ZhiAn in terror. Without a blink, Shen Lao continued telling his story.

Shen Lao may be in danger again, I thought. I knew I couldn't allow that to happen. "Shen Lao, could we continue our class next Friday? I forgot to turn off the centrifuge in the laboratory and must go right now." I stood abruptly and nudged ZhiAn. Silently, Shen Lao followed us out. We all realized that our class might be suspended for a while; however, none of us knew it would be the end of our Happy English Hour forever.

Later, I learned that the Red Guard had heard rumours about our secret English lesson and became curious. It was a close call. Thanks to the dimness of "the Coffin," we were not caught. What a lucky escape!

It was dear Shen Lao, a great teacher, who took the political risk to teach me. The class ended, but I've cherished the memory of our Happy English Hour ever since. And the good habits of reading and writing have stayed with me and will remain with me for the rest of my life. I still regret never seeing Shen Lao again after I left China in 1987 to emigrate to Canada, although we often wrote to each other.

In 1999, I moved to Toronto, to work in the Department of Biochemistry at the University of Toronto. A few years later, to my astonishment but also great joy, I discovered that Shen Lao had obtained his Ph.D. in 1946, in this very department! I even found his Ph.D. thesis in the department's library. What a happy coincidence! Since he was such a humble person, he never talked about this personal achievement or his experiences abroad. None of us knew about it. Standing in the middle of the library and holding his thesis, I felt a warmth flooding into my heart. "Thank you, Shen Lao." These were the only words I could utter through my tears.

Shen Lao died in 1992, after living for an eventful 92 years. Nevertheless, he left me his rich heritage of knowledge, his wonderful experiences, and his true love for us students and for the world. I promised myself that I would follow his example to teach and help my students in the same selfless way he taught me.

SWIRLING LEAVES
by Linda Torney

JAKE CAUGHT A GLIMPSE of movement out of the corner of his eye and glanced out the restaurant window. A gust of spring breeze had caught a small heap of last autumn's dried leaves. Trapped in a corner of the courtyard, they swirled in an eddy, circling higher and higher, until a single leaf reached the level of the eaves, where it hung suspended for a moment before spiralling gently back to the pavement. He watched, mesmerized, as the breeze caught it, and again sent it on its upward journey.

"Hey, man, you OK?"

He jerked his attention back to the plate of bacon and eggs in front of him. Manny had paused with a forkful of waffle midway to his mouth, his eyes quizzical.

"Yeah. Sorry. Mind was somewhere else for a minute there. What were you saying about the trip?"

"We pick up the canoes at Smoke River. Stay overnight in the motel and make an early start on Sunday. The rental company will truck a canoe carrier to the other end to meet us the following Saturday."

"How do we get back to the cars?"

"We'll take four vehicles for the six of us, and drive in convoy. Tony and Max will leave theirs at the pullout point. Then they can drive us and all our equipment back up to Smoke River afterwards to pick up the other two vehicles."

"Sounds good. Who's organizing the supply list?"

"Tony is. He said he'd have it done by next Friday. We can meet for a beer after work and divvy up the shopping." Manny glanced at his watch. "Hey, I have to run. I promised Megan I'd pick her up at two."

"You go on," said Jake. "I'll get the tab."

"Thanks, man. On me next time."

Manny grabbed his leather jacket and hurried out of the restaurant. Jake finished the last piece of bacon and reached for the pot to top off his coffee. He glanced out the window. The restless leaves were at it again, swirling up, drifting down, swirling up, drifting down.

"They're trying to escape," thought Jake. "But they can't. Something invisible has them fastened down. Sort of like me, tied to my boring job and mundane life."

A sudden chill ran up his spine. He gave himself a little shake and finished his coffee in a single gulp. It was unlike him to wax poetic over a pile of dead leaves. Besides, he had his mundane life to get back to—laundry and grocery shopping, and the stack of files he had brought home from the office. He signalled for the check.

Outside, he hurried toward his car, shivering in his light windbreaker. The deceptive March sun had caused him to forego his winter parka, but the wind was still cold enough to warrant it. "Hope it warms up some before the canoe trip," he thought. As he climbed into the car he glanced over at the deserted restaurant patio. The drift of leaves was still dancing its endless spiral.

At five in the afternoon on Friday, Jake packed up his briefcase and hurried over to the Keg restaurant. Tony, Max and Manny were already settled into a corner banquette, three pitchers of beer and six glasses invitingly lined up before them. Greg and Al burst through the door as Jake was shedding his coat.

"Aah, TGIF," said Al, pouring himself a beer. "And only three weeks to the great adventure."

Greg reached past him for the pitcher. "Speaking of that, I have a slight problem," he said. "My cousin is arriving in town a few days before we leave and planning to stay all the next week.

Normally, I'd just hand him the keys to the apartment, but he's here to finalize my aunt and uncle's estate. The last few months have been rough on him, and I think he's counting on my company. I hate to miss the trip, but..."

"Can he paddle?" asked Tony.

"Are you kidding? Born and raised in Muskoka."

"Then bring him along. Probably do him good to get into the great outdoors."

"It will mean an odd man," said Greg.

"Well, if you drop out, it's still an odd man," said Tony. "Either way, we'll have to equip one of the canoes with a passenger seat. If you don't come, we're down to five men and two canoes. But if you bring your cousin along, we'll be seven men in three canoes. It will be easier to distribute the equipment load."

"Are you sure?" asked Greg. He glanced around the table. "Everyone else okay with it?"

Heads nodded.

"Thanks, guys, I appreciate it. My cousin's name is Brian. I'll call him tonight."

Three weeks later, just after dawn on a sparkling Sunday morning, three canoes pushed off into the swirling current. Smoke River was running high after more than a week of rain, but today promised sunshine and clear skies. Jake, paddling stern in the middle canoe with Manny in the bow, breathed in the crisp air and felt a thrill of excitement at the beginning of the long-planned adventure.

He hadn't been in a canoe for awhile, but it all came back to him: the slide of silver water under the hull, the droplets falling from the paddle blade, the welcome pull of his muscles as he executed a j-stroke.

They stopped at noon for a sandwich lunch. At four they pulled the canoes onto a sandy patch of riverbank and pitched the tents. The campfire that first night was a noisy affair. Jake drank too much brandy, and suffered for it all the next day.

By Tuesday, their third day, the seven men had swung into an easy rhythm.

"How about that," crowed Tony. "Breakfast, breaking camp, and on the river in under half an hour."

"Yeah, but I forgot to pee," wailed Al, who was paddling stern in Tony's canoe.

"Aw, just hang it over the side," called Greg from the

passenger seat in the second boat. They were taking turns at the slacker's seat, as they had come to call it. The men's laughter cut through the morning fog hanging over the river.

"I guess this is where the name "Smoke River" comes from," said Jake, surveying the thick white wall.

"It will burn off by noon," called Max from the bow. He and Jake were third canoe in line.

The dense fog was hypnotic. Jake, already in an almost trance-like state himself, gradually became aware of the silence around him. The others had also fallen under the spell of the fog. All conversation ceased; their paddling took on a rhythm that seemed to match the slow pace of the river's flow. Even the birds were quiet. The dip-splash of the paddles making the only sound in this strange white world.

It must have been some time before he realized he was hearing a different noise. The sound of water. Fast moving water. He stopped paddling.

"Max, do you hear that?"

Max rested his oar and turned to look at Jake.

"It sounds like rapids," he said. "There isn't supposed to be white water on this part of the river."

They both looked ahead. Tony and Al's canoe had already vanished into the fog. Brian, Manny and Greg were shadowy silhouettes some meters away.

"Hey guys." The two shouted as one.

Brian half turned towards them, then snapped forward as another yell shattered the calm, this one edged with fear.

"Look out! Back paddle, back paddle!"

Jake saw Manny point, and the canoe ahead swung left, picking up speed.

"They're closer. We'd better take our direction from them," said Max. They put their backs into their oars.

It seemed an eternity to Jake, but was probably only minutes before they broke through the mist. A hellish scene lay before them.

Tony and Al's overturned canoe spun in an enormous eddy which lay square in the middle of the river. Tony, clinging to the canoe, circled with it. Al was nowhere to be seen. The second canoe stood off the edge of the vortex, Brian and Greg back paddling furiously in an effort to keep the nose free of the sucking water. Manny leaned far out over the bow, trying to get the tip of his paddle

within Tony's reach.

"Swing around!" yelled Max. "We'll try and get him from the other side."

Before Jake could react to Max's command, the side of the eddy broke in a wild churn of water, ten feet in front of their canoe. Al's head and shoulders shot above the surface of whirlpool, one hand waving frantically.

"Jesus!" cried Max. "Hand me the spare paddle. I'll try and get it to him"

Jake shoved the paddle within Max's reach, but it was too late. With a gurgling cry, Al sank beneath the surface.

"Tie the bow rope to it," yelled Jake. Max scrambled to secure the slippery nylon to the paddle, and rested the oar across his knees, scanning the water ahead.

"There he is! Al, Al, this way!"

Max took careful aim and flung the paddle out into the centre of the circling water.

"Are you guys nuts? The eddy's too strong! He'll pull you in with him!"

Jake heard Brian's shout and glanced over at the other canoe, where Manny still hung precariously over the bow, paddle outstretched to the circling Tony. For a split second, everything seemed frozen, the three men in the other boat, caught in action poses, all staring at Max and Jake's canoe in horror.

"They're right," he thought, his heart lurching into his throat, and he began to back paddle as hard as he could.

It was too late. Al had somehow managed to grab the bobbing oar, and with whatever strength he had left, was pulling himself back, inch by inch, along the rope. But for every inch Al gained, the canoe edged closer to the swirling eddy, until it reached the point of no return. The combined drag of the rope and force of the current tipped the boat. Its load of gear slid sideways, altering its centre of gravity, and the canoe overturned, flinging its contents, including Jake and Max, into the whirlpool's maw.

Jake found himself in the grip of a tremendous force, which spun him and pulled him at the same time. Desperate to free himself, he kicked and clawed his way to the surface, and sucked in a lungful of air before the monster seized him, hurling him against canoes and pieces of camping equipment. He struggled upward, only to be dragged back. This time, he lost his sense of direction and found himself clutching at rocks and deadfall on the bottom of the river.

Choking from panic and lack of air, he kicked off in the opposite direction. In the far distance, over the roar of the water, he thought he could hear shouting, Lungs bursting; he headed towards the faint sounds. Now he could see the water's surface. Whimpering, he reached out for it.

The gunwale of an overturned canoe struck him a glancing blow on the side of the head. Jake gasped, water flooded his lungs, and his world faded to black.

Then he was *above* the water. Below him, men and equipment and canoes circled down the steep sides of the eddy, while he seemed to be spiralling upward, the river receding below him.

"How can that be?" he asked himself.

Back in the courtyard of the café, a handful of dried leaves spiralled skyward in a sudden gust of wind. They drifted back to earth, where the wind seized them again. And again. And again.

An excerpt from the novel
KANISHKA
by Edwin Vasan

ON A DARK MOONLESS night Ramesh Kumar parked his pick-up truck about half a mile from his modest two-bedroom home. Normally he would back the truck into the shed that Manju allowed him to use at night before he walked home. Manju owned the only tea stall in town, which also doubled as a convenience store, with a shed that adjoined it.

Tonight, Ramesh wasn't going home. He was going to give the truck a quick cleaning before he drove to the city. He would stay for a couple of days with his brother Satish and his wife Dipa so that he would be ready to meet his son Ravi at the train station when he arrived. He'd spend the time in town catching up on family and doing some shopping. He'd phoned Satish a few days ago and told him that he would most probably drive in tonight so that Satish could leave the front door unlocked and Ramesh wouldn't have to wake anyone up late at night. The traffic would be relatively sparse and he should be able to make the trip in less than two hours.

He smiled as he thought about his son coming home. He had worked hard to put him through school and he was proud of Ravi's academic performance. All his report cards showed marks of over eighty-five percent and he often pondered on what Ravi might want

to do now that he had finished with his school. Engineering would mean a hard and challenging life at one of the IITs if he passed all the stringent entrance requirements. Medicine would mean a long and costly period of study before he... his thoughts were harshly interrupted by a stern voice.

"Kumar!"

He turned around and saw three ghostlike figures in the dark.

"Kaun? (Who is it?)"

"How long did you expect us to be patient you fool? It's been over three months and we haven't seen any money."

"I know. I'm sorry but I had to pay for Ravi's final year at school and his ticket home left me short. I promise I'll have something next month."

"Always next month, next month, next month. No more next month's for you now."

"Please, you have to understand. I..."

"What the fuck do I have to understand Ramesh?" a new voice interrupted.

Ramesh strained his eyes to see the new figure; one he knew well. One he was terrified of Chandu, the money-lender.

"Chandu saab! Give me just a month more and I will repay you all that I owe for the past few months. Please."

"You must think me a complete idiot Ramesh. If you have not been able to afford a month's payment where the hell will you find the amount for four, no five months?" Chandu snarled.

"Take him to the old temple and break a couple of his fingers," he instructed his three goons. "That should motivate him"

"No! Let's take him to his house and motivate his wife as well!"

Laughter erupted around him as all of them thought it would be a great idea. Ramesh knew he had to do something before they humiliated and hurt both him and his wife. He had to fix this problem. Soon.

The three henchmen grabbed him and pushed him into the back seat of the car they were driving. One of them sat beside him while the other two sat in the front and followed Chandu's car. Ramesh carefully scanned the inside of the car making sure he never moved his head. He had to get out. The car was speeding along the dirt road that led towards his house, past the abandoned temple, along the filthy pond past the only street light that had a mind of its own. On some days on, but usually off. Today was an on day and

as the car turned the last corner Ramesh noticed something shining on the floor below his feet almost hidden by the driver's seat. A screwdriver. Rusty, layered with dirt and oil it lay at the edge of his sandals. Ramesh jerked forward as the car hit another bump and reached down. Nobody noticed him grabbing the tool in the grinding, shaking dark. He pushed it under his legs and waited. A slim thread of hope but slim was all he could gamble on.

Suddenly, the driver slammed on the brakes and the car came to a grinding, creaking halt. No stealth here! Ramesh's door was opened by the driver.

"Out!"

"Please! Let me talk to my wife before you hurt us. Please. I beg you!"

"Out *madar-chodh*! Now!"

Ramesh waited for his backseat guard to get out through the other door. Hearing that door open he moved as if to get out and plunged the screwdriver as hard as he could into the driver's stomach. A sharp cry and blood spurting onto his hand. He pushed him aside and ran.

Gasping in panic and fear he prayed for some miracle to save him. All he heard was swearing and the sound of running. The sound of his feet? He turned. Chandu smiling. A gun. Chandu fired at Ramesh... Reverberation. Silence.

Ravi's train proudly rumbled into the Baroda railway station almost on time. He pressed his face against the dirt and insect-stained glass window and scanned the waiting sea of humanity on the platform amidst the red uniforms of the *coolies*, porters, the stray mongrels and the odd cow lying on the ground with no concern for the action. As the train squealed to a stop, Ravi still couldn't find his father and wondered if he had decided to wait outside. Parking problems. He picked up his only piece of luggage and joined the line-up to the door of his compartment. As he reached the open door a gust of hot air mingled with the smell of a million pieces of rotting garbage greeted him in undying familiarity. He seemed not to notice as he walked with the crowd towards the entrance constantly searching for his dad.

Not a sign.

Suddenly a familiar face. Uncle Satish. He looked at Ravi with a concerned and nervous look mingled with relief. Relief that lasted just a moment. Something wasn't right! Ravi's heart pounded louder and faster than usual and something told him that smiling and giving his uncle a big hug wasn't appropriate. Where was his

dad?

"Hello Ravi," Satish whispered. "I'm glad you had a safe ride."

"Where's dad?"

"I'll explain in a minute. Let's find a taxi first."

"Taxi? Where are we going uncle?"

"Our home."

Satish didn't say a word till they found a cab and reached his house in the city. He paid the taxi, picked up Ravi's bag and led the way in.

Satish's wife, Dipa, opened the door and it struck Ravi that she had been crying! Ravi had had enough.

"Aunty Dipa. I want to know what's going on! Now!"

"Ravi...," his uncle began

"Tell him Satish," Dipa sounded exhausted. "There's no point delaying the truth."

"Son, we have terrible news for you. Your parents are gone," Satish said.

"Gone. What the hell is that supposed to mean? Gone where?"

"There was an accident. A fire. The house burnt down while they were sleeping. They didn't have a chance. They probably didn't feel anything. The smoke would have killed them as they slept."

Little consolation.

"I'm sorry son. We both loved your dad and *bhabi* (sister-in-law)."

"What did they do with the bodies?"

"This happened a couple of nights ago. There is no morgue in Chalapur. They had to be cremated as soon as possible."

"Didn't someone have to write a report of some kind or something?" Ravi wasn't sure he was making sense but he didn't want to stop.

"The report was written at the police station and confirmed the cause of death Ravi."

"Can I go there and see the house? Talk to someone?"

"Of course. First thing tomorrow."

Satish was about to tell Ravi to get some sleep as it was getting late but he knew that it would sound pointless. So he sat down and put his arm around him.

Ravi cried uncontrollably as reality slowly sunk in.

SANCTUARY

by Herb Ware

I'M STARTING A NEW novel but it's one of those days a writer despairs of. On waking, I discover that the distant noise outside is from city workers repairing the water main. That explains why I can't shower or shave, brush my teeth or have coffee.

It does not begin to explain my septuagenarian mother's sullen silence as she draws all the drapes, turning the house into a mute, twilight cavern. She ensconces herself in her favourite living room chair and sets about silently reading another of those outdated brooding Victorian romances.

Her oppressiveness and the water main construction prompt me to phone a friend and invite myself over for the day.

My friend offers the backyard of her townhouse as a writing refuge. Not overly large, it's a perfect environment: stone slab patio with chairs; a long-poled umbrella piercing a wide table for my laptop; a surrounding, gated, two-meter-high privacy fence; and a plum tree whose branches overhang the fence's narrow top. While I work under the shade of the umbrella, my friend, cat in lap, lounges quietly reading in the shade of the fence.

It truly is a panacea, with only an occasional background

conversation from my friend to her cat. "Bubba, get down from there, you silly thing. Oh, kitty," she says sweetly, "how did you get into that tree? Aren't you the clever one, walking the fence?" They are a cute pair. She's a pixie-like creature who after a night at a Chinese buffet wouldn't top 100 pounds. On the other hand, Bubba, at 13 kilos, looks like a tie-dyed lynx. For a pampered cat, he has a surprisingly powerful physique – he's fast but also just a little bit clumsy.

While the two of them lounge, I focus my attention on the novel. In a short time I have written 200 words. The staccato Morse code of a nearby toy terrier barely registers as I concentrate. Yap-yap-yap. Yap-yip-yap-yap. I am equally able to ignore Bubba's responsive hiss while the dog's message and its master's counterpoint cursing, fade into the distance.

I connect another 50 excellent words into the panoply of paragraphs that will eventually generate an 80,000-word novel which is now one three-hundredth complete.

I take a break as Bubba leaps from the fence onto my head, sprawling me across my laptop's keyboard.

"Bubba," my friend chides gently. "You shouldn't disturb him like that," she coos and, with a weightlifter's grunt, hauls the feline from the table then heads back to her shady nook.

"You must have frightened the poor thing when you screamed," my friend admonishes while soothing the traumatized cat who in its near catatonic state hangs over her arm like a bath towel.

As I pull my shredded collar from the bloodied slits on my neck, Bubba raises his head and flicks his right paw in a single-clawed salute.

From the screen, I remove several lines of consonants that appeared when my chest landed on the keyboard and, with a deep cleansing breath, I refocus on the novel. My words flow in a sing-song pattern, just like the twittering of the flock of sparrows now lining the fence.

"Ah, well, if you get lemons…" I write the birds into my story, studiously ignoring their screaming flight as Bubba learns that it is possible to leap from lap to tree to fence — and beyond. His yowl as he slides off the narrow fence top barely scratches my creatively flowing mind. The sound of the squeaking fence gate and the frantic "OH MY GAWD!" however, does etch my concentration, as my friend rushes out to see if her feline survived the fall.

Bubba takes her approach as a game of chase and lights out for the bushes. With the two of them now occupied, I re-acquaint myself with the words on my laptop's screen. I take a no-nonsense approach to the story, planting the seeds for the sub-plot that will unfold in the beginning of the second chapter.

The sub-plot has nothing to do with the flash of wings that I note out of the corner of my eye so I carefully ignore the fence full of mourning doves that now lounge at my back. One side-steps into my line of vision, cocks its head appraisingly at the laptop screen. After a moment it slowly flicks its wing and, in a hollow, whistlingly mournful tone declares, "coo-hoo." Its companions take up the same critique: "coo-hoo, coo-hoo, coo-hoo."

I swing my arm in an overhead arc and the flock takes to the air, performs a beautifully executed formation loop and lands once more to continue its group critique of my work.

Bubba rescues me from the avian critics by performing a ground-to-air leap, sending the flock scattering to more friendly territory. Bubba also misses his landing and continues over the fence to light on my head, claws fully extended and with every intent of coming to a full stop. My flailing arms belatedly change his mind and he bounds to the far end of the table, where his mistress, lighting from the gate passage, scoops him up protectively and gentles his frazzled nerves with a cooing, "Naughty pussy, you shouldn't jump on those birds like that." Her mumblings into his ear are muted by his deep-bellied, broken-muffler purr as they make their way back to her shaded lounge chair.

Though blood is oozing lightly from my scalp, I'm left once more in peace. Beyond the fence, a city bus air-brakes its way to a halt at the nearby stop sign. I note the time on my laptop, 4:20 p.m., confirming the bus whose route frequency goes to five-minute intervals during rush hour. The revving drone of the bus's acceleration through the intersection is hardly noticeable because of the approach of a black, late model Cavalier. I can see its approach through the open gate, not that I need a sightline to know it's there; it came loaded with fully functional quadraphonic 600-watt speakers. I feel the hair on my head flattening to its dissonant head-banger chords.

Bubba too takes exception to the noise, flattening his ears and hissing at a decibel slightly less than the speakers. My friend reaches over and belatedly shuts the gate, eliminating at least one decibel of the fence-shaking sound just before the tire-squealing

music machine rockets off into someone else's space. Peace inflates itself like a dark, solitary bubble and my story once more re-forms in the belly of that calming.

The airplane's shadow does not disturb me, although its turbines grind threateningly as it banks for a landing at the near-by international airport. Did I mention that my friend lives under a flight path?

Not as quiet as the international flight is the teen on the skateboard who rhythmically thumps along the sidewalk imitating the da-tacka-da-tacka-da-tacka-da-tacka of a passenger train. It becomes cacophonous as his trailing buddies rush up in compounding cadence: tack-tackata-tadack-tack-tack-tackadacka.

That is not nearly so disturbing as the sudden silence signalling their liftoff from the curb and subsequent jump into the middle of the intersection to the squeal of wheels and a blaring horn. In that chaos the expletives that follow from all sides are barely noticeable – except to my friend. She makes quiet comment to Bubba about people's language as she looks in my direction.

"I was just trying out a phrase my character is going to say," I lie. Unlike the skateboarders, my lie crashes and burns.

I manage another 200 words in the sullen silence that follows. The tone of my story is taking an interesting turn toward the macabre just as a black squirrel makes a dash for freedom across the fence top. Bubba, taking exception to blatant invasion of his territory, leaps from my friend's lap onto the table, and tangles in my arms as they fly up to protect my already bloodied dome. Being Bubba, the cat doesn't apologize as he frees himself, and uses my face as a springboard in pursuit of the panicked nut hunter.

As I wipe my bloodied face, and carefully clean the scratches all over my arms, I explain how the day has been so successful that I have been able to achieve 550 words in mere hours, thanks to my friend kindly lending me her private space. She mumbles unenthusiastically about my being welcome anytime. Bubba, having returned from his pursuit, takes a tentative swipe at my head from the fence top as I exit through the gate.

When I get home, the austere, shadowy silence of the curtained living room wraps itself around me. My mother looks up from her book and offers a welcoming smile. I walk over and, sighing contentedly, hug her.

FLIGHT OF THE HORSE
by Karol Zelazny

I WAS SENTENCED TO be a milkman's horse for the rest of my life. The sentencing panel was made up of just one unshaven man, whose bad breath still lingers in my nostrils. This unlikely judge condemned me without charge or indictment, when he muttered with his toothless mouth, "Strong son of a bitch; farmer's special this one."

Consequently, I was sold to a milkman. Every day, morning and night, I pulled that milk wagon up and down the streets. It felt as if I pulled it through eternity! Hell! It felt as if I pulled eternity itself! Time stood still as I passed small, dirty houses, making my way through the town streets, like a ghost about to disappear into the twilight.

I was three years old and strong as a bull. I knew I was so much faster than any of the other horses running around the yard with me. Someone even remarked that I looked like a racehorse. At night, alone in my stall, leaving behind the mind-numbing drudgery of my day job, I escaped to a different life. I will never forget those wonderful dreams! I ran like a mad dog on the outside of a racetrack. The last quarter was approaching fast. I looked so

beautiful. All my muscles appeared to be playing in perfect harmony under my shiny black skin, almost ripping it apart, like a perfectly tuned New Orleans' jazz band from a bygone era. I never lost a race. Night after night I won the grand prize, receiving a long ovation from the people in the stands. Elegant women looked at me with admiration.

In the morning I would be hitched once again to the old milk wagon. The milkman's name was Zak Bialko.

Yes, *that* Mr. Bialko! I think you have heard that name, the world's most famous contemporary painter and sculptor, who established the undercurrent of today's art. Zak Bialko, the man who created the world's first political party, whose main goal was to teach people to participate in world affairs through art. In the eyes of many, he was a giant among us. During the time in which I knew him, he was just another unhappy man. The difference was, Zak fully realized his demeaning situation and never accepted it, while others were only too happy to be served scraps left over from the party of the gods.

Zak, a married man, had two little kids who he loved dearly, although from the outside, it was difficult to spot any signs of this love. I was often an unwilling witness to the pushing and yelling Zak administered to his kids, for crimes against humanity they were guilty of. Many times I could see his eyes fill with desperation. More than once, he took his anger out on me. I didn't mind. I had thick skin and a little pain always helped me to forget the malignant thoughts that were plaguing me.

My fourth birthday was approaching fast, and the pain of the unfulfilled, empty, meaningless life I was carrying inside, became unbearable. There was a big "Stop" sign at the end of my road. My earthly trekking was coming to a screeching end, as I quickly mapped out a plan that I would put into action, at the first opportunity. Zak did not have the slightest idea of my intentions. Had he suspected, I'm sure he would have kissed me on the mouth. My plan was quite simple. There was a grocery store at the top of the hill! I planned to pull slowly up to that point, and then fly down the hill with the speed of a hurricane, right into the centre of the town. Just thinking about it gave me shivers of pleasure. In my mind's eye I could see the wonderful panic my raid would cause, with milk cans rolling off the wagon, creating a true "Milky Way" behind me. People would dive for cover in a futile attempt to avoid the madness. I hoped that Zak would be thrown off the wagon during this wild ride and

smash his poor head against a merciful telephone pole, ending his pathetic life. I also aimed to cut down a couple of fire hydrants and for the grand finale, hit the gas station in the middle of town. My goal was to be blown to pieces by the explosion, or to die in the resulting fire.

I successfully executed my plan. Memories of these events are still fresh in my mind as I warm up for yet another race. Sometimes, I miss my friend Zak, but the excitement of the coming race eases this feeling. I did see Zak a couple of weeks ago, after being separated from him for almost a year. He waved to me from the stands as I was preparing for another race. He changed a lot. He is now a smiling, confident man. Attached almost permanently to his arm is a pretty, tall blonde. His wife. A nice transformation when compared to the bony, sad and angry person she used to be.

I, too, have changed quite a bit. I have become the fastest stallion on the racetracks of the world. I have been awarded countless trophies and other prizes. My friend, trainer and owner, Mike Dunn, has received piles of cash for races I have won.

My new name is "Running Thunder," and I rather like it. The change in my lifestyle is radical and it clearly reflects my crazy deed. I had implemented my plan perfectly, save for a few details. Half of the town burned to the ground after the explosion at the gas station. Many people lost their lives, others — only their earthly possessions. Zak landed softly in a ditch and ended his milkman's career with a bump on his forehead. Myself, I hadn't a scratch on me!

They called me "The Mad Horse," and a local butcher started to sharpen his biggest knife, but meanwhile, Mike, my present owner, unexpectedly found himself visiting our town. He looked me over, and said the most beautiful words I have ever heard in my entire life. Until the day I die, I will always remember these words. He said, "You can't force a race horse to pull a milk wagon. No wonder he went mad," he added. Mike then took me to his stables, and after a brief training period, I started to race.

I have won most of the races in which I have taken part. You ask: "How is it possible?" Simple. Every time another horse tries to pass me, I start thinking about my life as the milkman's horse. The emotions I feel transform me into a running thunder. Nobody can keep up. Once I overheard someone say, "That horse flies," and that is an accurate description of my performance.

As for Zak? The bump on his head served him well. Some-

thing moved inside him. Some force was awakened. He locked himself in a god-forsaken damp and dilapidated basement for six months after the accident, and poured his dark soul into the one picture he painted during that time. The painting was later purchased by some wealthy Bostonian and donated to the Boston Museum of Art. Thousands of visitors come daily to see it. They all stand there in front of it; silent, astonished, amazed! If you ask me, the painting is okay, I think. I'm not an art critic, but it's still considered to be Zak's greatest achievement. The thing I like most about it, is the title: *Flight of the Horse*.

An excerpt from the memoirs "The other I"
THAT DEADLY EXHALE!
by Zohra Zoberi

'EELAY EEFAY' MEANS THE centre of learning and culture, the hub of the Universe. According to the Pagan belief, this is where mankind originated. This small Western Nigerian town in Yuroba land met with its newfound fortune when it was selected as the ideal site to build the largest university campus in that oil rich country. Before the dream of this centre of learning and culture could fully materialize, a temporary campus next to Ibadan University was set up.

My husband was hired at a handsome salary and generous fringe benefits. As the newlywed teenage wife of a University Professor, I was quite excited to inherit a spacious, fully furnished bungalow situated in the midst of the 'Flame of the Forest.' These lush, green, tall trees with tamarind like leaves laden with bright red flowers, as though in full bloom for my reception, formed a beautiful canopy over the rooftop of our bungalow. In this hub of the universe, inside that bungalow, we were surrounded with colourful happiness.

Surprisingly, I turned out to be a novelty to this multi-national community of mostly elderly professors and their wives.

Their children were left behind in their countries of origin and only visited their parents in Nigeria during summer vacations. I was therefore, the youngest one around and available to be pampered at will.

It is only now that I have acquired my status as a mature woman better termed as a 'Golden Girl' that I can fully realize why they were fascinated with my arrival. Youth is so attractive to the elderly. The first dinner in honour of the 'Youngest Bride on the Campus' was given by Jeoffrey and Rolly, an English couple who wanted to welcome me. It felt great to be the guest of honour where everyone else was at least twice my age. I vowed to be on my best behaviour for the occasion.

My taste buds were trained for *achaar and chatnee* (spicy pickles) — flavours I hungered for. The aroma of the delectable 'Qorma' (fancy beef curry with delicate herbs) or that Basmati rice with saffron and cinnamon were now just a dream. Instead, the four-course dinner menu that evening included green pea soup and liver pate. Though I can handle it now, back then that thick green soup reminded me of my little siblings' baby poop and the liver pate more like... Nonetheless, I took on this challenge whole-heartedly and despite the urge to throw up, I managed to competently gulp it down. I even mimicked everyone else by saying "It's so delicious".

From the corner of my eyes, I secretly observed everyone else in order to choose the right fork and the appropriate knife for each course. I found it impossible to balance those miserable little slippery peas at the back of my fork. My husband, having lived in England for a decade, could do it quite comfortably. Uh-huh, so he did have an edge over me! My main agenda was to show him that I wasn't just a sheltered teenager from a little town of Rawalpindi, that I knew it all.

After dinner, our host presented a cigarette to a smartly dressed European lady who was sitting beside me. I found her mannerisms highly impressive and worth emulating. Gracefully accepting the cigarette offered to her, she bent forward with a noticeable style. The host lit her cigarette and she leaned back with a relaxing inhale, followed a few seconds later by a gentle exhale.

I observed it all. The host then offered me a cigarette. I gracefully bent forward, copying each and every motion of that stylish lady, including the way I crossed my legs and tilted my head. And I inhaled! Surprisingly enough, I didn't cough even once. How I felt was a different matter. In spite of the dizziness and

nausea, I was so proud of myself, ever more determined never to let my partner down.

I noticed that my husband remained silent throughout the evening — that being one of his positive traits, initially I ignored it. Once I glimpsed the sadness on his face, I became concerned that he might in fact not be feeling well. It was only on the way home, when he hardly answered me, that I realized there was a good possibility that he was upset with me which was a shock in itself. How could anyone be upset with me? No one ever was! After my repeated requests he reluctantly uttered a few words, "Do you really have no idea what's bothering me?"

"I don't, really I don't." I vehemently pleaded my innocence. He then told me how disappointed he was that I hadn't noticed his disapproval of my smoking that cigarette. He was utterly shocked and had no idea that I was a smoker.

"I swear to God that it happens to be the first cigarette I ever smoked in my entire life," I vowed.

I convinced him of my sincere intentions to please him — for that, I was willing to go to any length. For my skilful participation in the smoking event, in my mind I had deserved a pat on the back. He, on the other hand, told me he was sad to realize that he had left some gorgeous English girl behind in order to marry a traditional Eastern girl from Pakistan, only to find out she's a chain smoker. With difficulty I swallowed my pride, pleaded for forgiveness and explained that I only did this to impress him. I then requested he at least appreciate my adaptable nature. That seemed to do it, he finally forgave and I thought the issue was resolved.

I then dwelt on who this 'gorgeous' English girl he had sacrificed over me was! I recalled his photo album in which there was a pretty lady with curly locks and a frilly frock. *What an old fashioned woman* I consoled myself with that observation. And what was she holding in her right hand? A cigarette!

PART TWO
POETRY

MOVING WATERS
by John Ambury

From distant springs clear trickles start
sparse waters flow, drink rain and swell, connect in brooks
collect in streams, become a river
in quiet drift and headlong flight
a life.

Your river comes from all its streams
components, colours, temperatures, threads
united but not uniform
one river of many waters.

My river is from different springs
as complex and as separate yet inseparable
as multi-hued and varied
as calm where wide and slow, as turbulent in wilful flood as yours.

Our rivers meet.
They clash and turmoil, streams conflict, repel
too many parts, the parts not made to fit
I am not yours to absorb, you will not yield to my flow
we are not one, my warmth is cold to you
and yet, my blue reflects your green
your green takes in my blue
one day my warmth gives warmth to you
at last we join and move together
united though not uniform
the sum of all our waters.

After the delta will be the end, the silent end
no longer us nor any thing
the cosmic blank, the emptiness
of nothing.

But before that, love, before!
we'll gently spread through meadows

slow and tranquil, embracing love as flowers
we'll rage through canyons, rough-walled, deep, confining
but cannot hold our boundless power
surging in rapids, white-water
shouting love as passion
overcoming, explosive, wild
then calm again.

One river of all waters, we flow and thrive
we feed the earth and nurture, we take and we destroy
we are nature, alive and primal, relentless
sweeping to the delta
to the end.

THAT I CAN GIVE
by John Ambury

Take what I have that I can give
Don't look for moon or stars
Or diamond's glint
Or gold

Take what I have that I can give
Don't look for faithful bliss
Or soul all yours
And true

Take what I have that I can give
The part I've torn away
From other lives
For you

Take what I have that I can give
The part I keep for you
That small, bright shard
I've saved

Take what I have that I can give
The fire within my heart
My longing need
My flesh

Take what I have, my love, that I can give
The part that's yours, the part that makes me live.

SCARBOROUGH BLUFFS
by N. Patricia Armstrong

tall they stand
measuring time
in thousand-year slices
long clay fingers
reach to touch
glimmering sky

enveloping ice
etched gashes into
unresisting sand
retired and left
creviced wounds
to heal in tropic warmth

grains of sand
sands of time
sandsong sad song

sturdy young legs
span dusty clay
running shoes
slipping
sliding
across wide expanse
grope for twisted branches
hug the broad
cliff-face
bleeding knees
stinging hands
down
down
down
forbidden trails
to patiently
waiting
beach

grains of sand
sands of time
sandsong sad song

wooden matches snick
into ruby flame
nostrils burn with
sulphur's acrid bite
wieners
writhe and sizzle
on crooked sticks
fresh sharp zing
of
yellow mustard
bites the tongue
savouring the
first
wild
taste
of blackened meat
orange pop swigged
from brown-ribbed bottles
dribbling
down
sunburned
chins

grains of sand
sands of time
sandsong   glad song

shifting shadows
brush towering cliffs
blue-veined hands
brush falling tears
grains of sand
cross sands of time
intersect
swiftly
passing
years

measureless sands
infinite grains
each   a   universe complete
world within
world without
traversing
our
short
span
melt into
the   waiting   lake

LETTING GO
by Elizabeth Barnes

Clearly she'd been letting herself go
no more swims or daily walks
no more timed-concentration puzzles.
Now it was multiples of gin & tonic before dinner
and sugary desserts;
macaroni and cheese and bacon sandwiches,
and there was the endless line of cheap schmaltzy music
—as if she couldn't get enough.

She wore the house like a heavy cape
a carapace about her shoulders and back.
It breathed with her,
expanded and contracted,
shuddered and settled.

When she went to her bed,
mindless of the electricity bill,
she left the house ablaze,
all lights burning brightly, cheerfully, in their sockets,
light thrown carelessly against the darkness.

The cat confused by so much brightness
roamed the house, a restless ship
cruising the edges of the rooms. When asked
why this was happening to her,
she shrugged, was uninterested in finding an answer.

After years of struggling against mindlessness & disorder
she now sought it and with relish
let it flow over and through her.
So many tendrils of earthbound gravity.

She slept late,
undisturbed when the spring sun climbed thru the trees and into
her window

throwing patterns of lace and new leaves on the dusty walls,
the cat exhausted and curled in the crotch
formed by her disorganized legs.

STREET OBSERVATIONS
by Elizabeth Barnes

I.

It is over in an instant:
outside the liquor store,
he commands her to sit, and with
her bum half-way to the ground,
he yanks her leash and says, *No,*
sit here, on the other side of the
bike lock-up.

Glossy strawberry-blond,
she looks up beseeching,
tries to do the right thing,
young setter eyes unsure.

He is tall, dressed in darkness,
an American civil war cap on his head:
a man full of commands.
A voice & a shadow.

II.

Out of the sub-zero wind-chilled air,
snug in the doorway of a row house,
she, small and thin,
deep within a long woollen coat and knitted hat,
a burning cigarette clamped in her gloved fingers,
and he, patient in bulky parka and brown hunter's cap,
well-furred flaps secure over his ears and forehead,

sit as if it were always so.
Perhaps there was, to begin with,
a cup of weak tea and disjointed
but heart-felt conversation,

and maybe a few thin biscuits,
always followed, regardless of the weather,
by a perch on the narrow doorstep,
her cigarette burning in place.

As I pass by,
he peers up at me,
eyes meeting eyes,
from under the brim of his fur-lined cap,
and smiles, as if to say he knows, that I know, that
this is it,
their tacit arrangement,
which stretches backwards and forwards in time,
and is not to be questioned.

IS LOVE SO FRAGILE?
by Joan Chisholm

You are not here
And I don't know
If love exists

Though you have burnt my lips
With your fire and
Made my world shake with ecstasy

You arrive tomorrow
My body is tuning itself

A THOUSAND STARS
by Joan Chisholm

I cannot make you love me
But, I can wait
For you to recognize your beauty
And, the worthiness of you

When love selects your soul
Your world is lit up
By a thousand stars

Accept love
Give love
And take the world

TO A DREAM
by R. G. Condie

You floated in, a vision white and rose.
My quickening heart skipped beats in sheer delight,
With entire being reaching, stretching close,
To hold such fragile beauty through the night.
Each tender touch reduced me to a state
Where time and motion blurred before my eyes.
My mind resigned, accepting any fate,
And breathing simply stilled itself to sighs
What was this warmth pervading all of me,
Suffusing, scintillating, sibylline?
Who guessed the frightening force that love could be,
Or what the implications so unseen?
Ah memory which causes pulse to race.
Oh when again may I enfold such grace?

VAL DAVID
by Jasmine D'Costa

I stand on the street at Val David holding your hand
on the tired road beneath my feet.
In the distance, the hills blue-green stretching sleepily,
fade into distant colours.
Undoubtedly, the road ends there
And beneath endless pines, the forest path
is defined by the lone traveler
I look around for you
But all I see is the straight road to the hills
and nothing beyond

BURNING
by Jasmine D'Costa

1962, the Indo-China war,
I gazed through shaded windows into darkness
as sirens screamed, and the sky lit up with anti-aircraft fire
a hundred stars in the starless Bombay night
Four unscented candles stood on the floor
where I sat beneath the table
reading Tolstoy's *War and Peace*

Four scented candles burn, flicker, ignite
till it is time to get out of our bath
We take pleasure in fires
that eat into our oxygen
subduing such beauty
into molten wax on the cold marble floor

SPRING MORNING
by Josie Di Sciascio-Andrews

the dandelions have returned
like a million little suns

such childish diadems
bursting yellow rays of joy
on the dark fringed brow
of green may grasses
fragrant with the hope
of seemingly empty space
dark matter teeming
with possibilities of renewal

soon, their thin petal strips will fall
like short lived loves
their orgasmic sun bursts
replaced by downy puffs of seed
haloes of a million tiny candles
each homely flame an arrow
sharp like truths behind all pleasures
like children waiting to be birthed
beyond the falling stars of lust
burned off sparklers
extinguished suns
exchanging macroscopic incandescence
for the small smouldering
of bloomlessness
the uneventful life of ordinary days
left over in spades
of bitter foliage
after the brief bright joys
the memory of them
redeeming the rest
of the mundane existence
of the beautiless
rooted in the humble earth

NOCTURNE
by Josie Di Sciascio-Andrews

against blue darkness
tall pines
etch
ominous crystals
in the cave of night

their inverted roots
burrowing deep
shadows
in vast emptiness

north star, a pin
firm in its place
holds up the night
like a circus tent
above our town

I stand on
a velvet fold of karma
all unuttered thoughts
bouncing back
to their own source of gravity
such agile gymnasts
elastic on their trampolines
trapeze artists skimming tightropes
elephants, tigers
braving hoops of deathly flames
parades of human talent
beauties, frightening beasts
flaunting their tamed, glittered ferocities
each gift, each oddity
of the whole gaudy world
dangling
from ropes in midair
as an audience forever gasps

to the expected drum roll
we the acrobats
with our telltale garb
our own bejewelled limbs flailing
leaping towards other hands
blindly seeking
grasping at solid objects
in the ever growing possibility
of falling
without nets

LIGHT ON THE GROUND AND LIGHT IN THE MIND
by Mary Craig Gardner

Land itself dictates
what images metabolise from light
memory or imagination may unfold upon it.
I talk about dry land,   not land under the waters
in any case, not called land.
Rather, I think about that gritty, stony stuff
where our earthy selves walk.
I am thinking about land...
Land outside of the buildings we live and work in.
Land outside the cities, towns and villages.
Land as landscape which my cultural lenses tell me how to read.
Sometimes the lenses slip
being born English my memory starts cross fading
the green Ontario temperate parkland into English countryside.

On land is where most of us start our life's journey
Outside, landscapes change daily.
Only my memory landscapes are settled.
Remembered landscapes — images,
I notice their silence, their stillness

Images become words.
And   words bring on the images.
Which comes first, or does it matter?
In any case, you, my reader are even now forming your own
images from these words.

And so, to start not in England but in North America.
Still thinking about land
I cannot imagine North American land
without native North Americans.
Over the land silently, over the mighty waters lightly
in small vessels go the Dene and the Inuit.
Mayans, say they belong to the land, to Mother Earth.

This sacred cosmic connection, realised in stories
anoints the land with its perfume.
Mythic yes, but how they steady the land

And I cannot imagine North America without the rest of us -
imports like myself, or descendants of imports.

My imagination visited by recorded history - winter, 1793 -
sees the northern shore of lake Ontario
where the Simcoes freshly arrived from southern England
with their red coated soldiers
are living in their high sided tents
Their habitation for the cold, cold winters.
Their sailing ships, safely harboured nearby in Lake Ontario.
Lady Simcoe bears a child in this tent.
No roads. No net. No telephone. No radio. No aeroplanes.

Later adventurers arriving from Europe
flap legal documents under native noses.
Claim ownership of the land.
Suddenly, land is an image of personal wealth and prestige.
A very slanted kind of security.
How can one possibly own actual land?
Like the adventurers I once set out to own some land.
I bought ten acres.   Two weeks later I sold it.
I couldn't figure out my connection to it.
An attachment to England possibly blocked
the comforting gesture of ownership.
Ownership, governed by culture enables us to live together...
Sometimes.

THROUGH THE MIST OF TIME
by Zita Hinson

I could still touch and smell and feel
That unforgettable place in my mind
I remember the stillness of black velvet nights
Hot golden days so bright
There were no cold winter winds that bite

Just the touch of sunshine on my face
That soothed, and comforted like a warm embrace
The sound of rain falling on galvanized roofs
Lulling me to sleep
The feel of warm sand beneath my feet
Every new day a challenge, never a thought of defeat
I long for that time once more.

Through the echoes of my mind I still can hear
Children laughing, dogs barking, steel bands playing
Noise, heat, the calypso beat
I see flowers growing in wild profusion everywhere
Their fragrance filled the air
Colourful hibiscus, stately Palmist trees
Sugar cane plants swaying gently in the breeze
I long for that time of ease

It was a time of hoping, searching, anticipating
A time of innocence, a time that was real
It was a time of youthful pleasure, it now seems unreal
A time of dreams and laughter
Dreams of my knight in shining armour
Dreams of happiness ever after

That land so fair beyond compare
That time I long and yearn for
Alas is no more. It can no longer be mine
Yet it remains indelibly engraved on my mind
And there it will stay
Through the Mist of Time

THE HUG OF A CHILD
by David Kimel

How to contain the un-containable?
How to embrace the un-embraceable sea,
The dispersing fluid of clouds,
The ever moving winds,
The eternally penetrating light in dark
And a child's thirst for love?

With a hug he squeezes not just a body,
Not only a heart receiving his fervid breath
But the strength of an adult,
A sun drenched playground,
A world of happiness and plenty
And a promised universe of assurance.

In exchange we feel the softness of his hands
Tying the knot around our necks
And in this undisturbed show of love
We look scared that the world is not how he's seeing it
And our limitation is glooming the sun in his eyes.

LIFE

by David Kimel

Life, a flight of stairs
Spinning around in circle,
Evolving, year after year,
In spiral to other level,
And a different stage,
Like a Babylonian tower
Rising to an ever-foggy top.

On this spiral,
My weak feet are climbing
Steadily, tiredly,
On the growing path,
Pulling an already heavy, expandable,
Load of memories, regrets
And irremovable mistakes.

Ahead, steamy clouds become
Closer and inscrutable.
Behind, insignificant creatures
Swarm like ants, fast reeling
On a Lilliputian stage
I had the lead part.

WOUNDED
by Maria Pia Marchelletta

A morning mauled by moans
Among misty moors pallid faces flee
The mush mud and foliage in injured troughs
smells of sweet-scented blood. Fauna dead or absent.
In the ditch sprouts silence
with arms of steel; hiding vigilant eyes shout
and watch explosives steadily burst...
the mortals
will not sleep any longer

Mumbling and stumbling
whining cries of wounded
drip thorns of dark blood
straddling along like chained
convicts; despair and exhaustion
beat them down
fade into rows of crying crosses
The path like the journey
void of meaning; bitter sadness
swells up in their throats
The mortals don't sleep
here any longer

But I see them again ploughing along
the dirt road bandaged with blood
blinded by humble sainthood...
with splints and slings soaring
on wings of suffering
Amidst underground sleep
they will not weep
they will not be found
Since immortals now do not sleep
hardly any longer

SHADOWS
by Maria Pia Marchelletta

I am face to face with my shadow.
Paint a trail of lies and equinoctial tears.
I must take you back to my woodwork.
Pains of betrayal splinter my soul.
Now, you are here
try to tear open like a bubbling burst
of energy. As blooms on a flower bed, we burst
into a sparked shadow.
Utter half-truths with guilt and here
 bargain with truth and tear
secretly as my teacup fills with hope. My soul
builds a bridge to your woodwork.

Awaited desires sink into the woodwork.
Thirsty for emotions, songs burst
in white silence of the whole soul.
Your nameless soul sings in its shadow;
as an exposed meadow it drops tears
into my breath and you sink here.

All else is superfluous here.
You are rooted and unmoved woodwork.
Heaven-born you stay frozen in tears
like snow while spring bursts
come to greet your whitening shadow
which speaks and feels as a woman's soul.

You draw from others soul
and blend your golden hair with a green wreath, here.
Love lingers in the circle of your shadow.
Your beauty has more virtue than precious woodwork.
Your unhealed wounds still burst
with desire, and wear a crown of tears.

Release your fears and tears.

Like rivers flow to hills, let your soul
take fire for me and burst
into my life again, perhaps here
your form can spark love in my woodwork.
This love, I bear for your very shadow.

Sweet tears linger here
your wounded soul hides in my woodwork
as hills burst with your shadow.

INTOLERANT WEATHER
by Cassie McDaniel

From room to room,
we refrain from speaking.
Anything we said would light like fire
and we're sitting in a puddle of estrogens, much like fuel.

If we'd both witnessed tragedy
a tornado through our living room,
roaring nightmare cracking splinters
through our living room,
I'd say that I could fashion dinner from the canned goods.
You'd say that you could put the bags over the windows.
We'd make a home again, if it was someone else's fault,
but instead we fight, from room to quiet room.

Four, fluff and chirping, skin scratching feet,
nesting in their box of light, underneath the stairs
and you above them, nesting upstairs away from the static,
charging the air but not yet exploding,
gasping for some warmth.
You cuddle up against yourself,
devoid of down
and as we strain ourselves not talking
I wonder why no trees have yet been pummelled through our roof.
Do we not deserve it?

There is no chirping when we're warmer.
Night-time settles into the folds of a cardboard box, but not
comfortably,
and in our fluff and fury
through empty rooms, we hear again and again,
the sounds of condemnation.

THE RED IN POETRY
by Cassie McDaniel

It doesn't take much to be a poet
you need a red book
hide-away hide-out don't-look
warning, dangerous words
It doesn't take much.

It doesn't take much to be a woman
red mouth
red-words red-eyes look-out
heavy, breath like gravy
red gravy.

It doesn't take much to be a poet
you need a big hurt
deep pain, like Peguis canyon
in Mexico, off the main roads
swoop and dive, like a red-tail
arrogant and lost.

KALEIDOSCOPE
by Jatin Naik

We meet so many people,
Some of noble heart
They come and they go
something to give and something to take,
that's life!

We stay with each other for that moment in time,
Closely aligned,
And as years come and go,
we are left standing, alone,

Our lives, a shake of a Kaleidoscope,
That's how it goes,
Our lives, a shake of a Kaleidoscope,
That's what our destiny shows,

The meeting of old friends,
And events with a familiar trend,
as in a circular flow,
make our memories glow,

we move within the Kaleidoscope,
That's how it goes,
We move within the Kaleidoscope,
That's what our destiny shows!

SACRIFICE
by Jatin Naik

A candle burns out to brighten the room
And henna, churned to bring color
The setting sun lets stars shine,
And a warrior sacrifices his life silently!

A child's cries brings joy to its parents
and seeds blossom to bear fruits
Fruits ripen to satisfy hunger,
And a mother loves unconditionally!

A gardener trims the hedges to enhance beauty,
and bees toil to give nectar
The wind works away gloomy clouds,
And a social worker toils selflessly!

A roly-poly jokes about himself with others,
And a wise man enlightens
The old tell tales to their children's children,
And the clown brings hearty laughter!

A flower fades away sharing its fragrance,
and sugar amalgamates and sweetens
The drums soothe out lilting music with rhythm,
And those in love, do so truly!

A lily shoots out from marshy land,
And order emerges out of chaos
The seed germinates into a tree,
And the dreamer manifests his dreams painstakingly.

PEACEFUL GRACE
by Andrew Scott

As you prepare to take your walk into the light
You can hide your fear and take delight
In the mark you have left on this earth
A measure of your worth
You passed your strength on
the receivers knowing where they belong
have taken the lessons taught
And the knowledge sought
Your presence improved us all
As you now stand tall

Where you will be going
Inner peace is what you will be sowing
as we watch you quietly say goodbye
a touch of sadness in the corner of your eye
May your next destination
take away all of the world's frustrations
May you have a quiet journey through the hands of time
And may your tired heart always chime
So please take away the fear from your face
As in life, you will always walk with peaceful grace

THE OL' MAN IN THE MOUNTAIN
by Andrew Scott

Jack, an ol' man that lived in a mountain
Life came from him, like water from a fountain
He gave life to a family of four
A wife, that made up the perfect score
Together in a cabin that was poor
he had his family that is what his life was for

Jack a jolly ol'man, was all heart
He would go poor to give you a start
He was a sight to see
Orange hair, grey beard that almost reached his knee
You never heard him holler
His small body full of laughter

Pride and honour walked with him everyday
If you had honesty, he gave you the time of day
He would speak the truth when you did not want to hear it
But he picked the times when it would fit
When he considered you a friend
He would be beside you until the end

No one knew when the disease came
He wore it without shame
Jack's tanned skin went white
He would tell you he was alright
Even when Jack was at his weakest
He was full of tenderness

Friends and family paid respects when he was taken away
Remembering the joy Jack brought everyday
We celebrated his memory
While his frail soul was being set free
How we can see him in his own heaven
Laying peacefully, as the Ol' Man in the Mountain

BIOGRAPHIES
OF AUTHORS

JOHN AMBURY is a technical writer in Toronto who has recently turned his hand to fiction and poetry. Many of his short stories and poems have been posted on the internet, but (aside from sonnets in his high school yearbook) these are his first published works.

N. PATRICIA ARMSTRONG's poetry and short stories have been published in several anthologies. The poem presented here recalls her happy childhood memories at the *Scarborough Bluffs*. Patricia's book, *Geneamania - Would the right Christian Schneider please stand up?* will be released soon, and encapsulates her sixteen years' research of her Pennsylvania German ancestors.

ELIZABETH BARNES is a poet, writer, and an active member of the High Park Writers' Group. She was shortlisted for the Writer's Union of Canada short story contest for her story entitled *The Yellow Dahlia* in 2002. She works for the City of Toronto facilitating a creative writing and a fabric art group at a women's resource centre.

DAHN BATCHELOR was a nationally syndicated newspaper columnist and TV talk show host during the 1970s and 1980s. He has had several short stories published along with a number of articles and he is the author of several essays in business and medical journals. At 76, he is now working on his memoirs.

KATHLEEN BETTS is a contributor to the Napoleon Hill e-Zine and Good News Toronto, writing to inspire integrity and respect for humanity. Alumnus of UWO, Dale Carnegie, Toastmasters, Microskills, and Keep Any Promise, with her heart in Glengarry, Kathleen lives in Scarborough, Ontario.

YVONNE BLACKWOOD is an author, columnist and public speaker. Her published books include the very successful *Into Africa: A Personal Journey* ranked in the top five best-selling books under Ghana on Amazon.com in 2002 and the hilarious *Will That Be Cash or Cuffs?* Her third book *Into Africa: The Return* will be published fall of 2009.

ALISON E. BRUCE started writing stories at the age of twelve and hasn't stopped since. Copy writer and editor since 1992, she started working toward publication of her fiction at the insistence of her terminally ill sister, Joanne. Alison is a member of the Writers and Editors Network and Crime Writers Canada.

ALTUG CAKMAKCI is a member of High Park Writers Group and he is currently working on a novel. His two novels in Turkish, *Simdiki Zamanin Tarihi/History of Present Time* and *Renkli Taslarin Siyah Golgesi/Black Shadow of Coloured Stones*, were published in Turkey.

MAURO CAPPA's most recent publications include *Midnight Song Anthology of Verse, Earth to the Moon* (Vaughan Poets' Anthology) by Hidden Brook Press, and *Verse Afire* by Beret Days Press. His debut collection *Renderer of Words* is forthcoming by Joie de Plume Books in 2009. He is also the recipient of the Odette-Mohan Scholarship.

JOAN CHISHOLM is the author of *Dream Maker*, a paean to following one's dreams which was written from the experience of following her own dream of writing. Her literary work contains words of hope that set others free. She lives in Toronto, Ontario and is inspired by her city and its people.

CHRISTINA CLAPPERTON has been writing creatively for a year, practicing her craft in writing courses and groups and even summoned the courage to do a reading at the Words Alive Literary Festival. An excerpt from her novel *Stuck in Wonderland* received an Honourable Mention in the SLS Unified Literary Contest.

NANCY KAY CLARK is a magazine writer and editor. She is a gold winner at the National Magazine Awards and the recipient of numerous Canadian Business Press Awards. Nancy is a member of the Saturday High Park Writers Group and her short fiction was featured in the Saturday High Park Writers Group Anthology.

R. G. CONDIE is an author of five books, ghost writer, columnist journalist, poet and short story writer. He is Canadian Authors Association first Writer in Residence, editor, and mentor.

JULIET DAVY is an author, actress and educator who works with special needs children and youth. Her short story *Treasured Moment* was published in the *Food for Thought* anthology. Her work *The Path to Transformation and Forgiveness* was nominated for a top ten award in the *Dreamweavers* writing competition. Juliet also co-wrote and performed in the play *StreetHearts*.

JASMINE D'COSTA is an accomplished Toronto author. Her recent publications include a collection of short stories *Curry is Thicker than Water* by BookLand Press. Jasmine just completed her first book of poetry *A Million Pieces of China* and currently working on her novel *Saving Ali*. From banker to writer, her mind is one large whirl of words and stories waiting to be written.

SUSAN DESVEAUX is a health care/medical research worker and Reiki Master, born and raised in Toronto. She has a background in theatre performance, production and design and has written poetry, plays and short stories. Susan is currently working on her first medical mystery novel.

SALLY DILLON is a freelance writer residing in Toronto, Ontario. She has had her short stories published in *More Memoirs Around the Table*. Sally is presently working on a book portraying her memoirs about growing up in a small Ontario town. In her time out from writing Sally enjoys gardening, swimming and practicing the marital art of Taoist Tai Chi.

JOSIE DI SCIASCIO-ANDREWS was born in Italy an emigrated to Canada at the age of 13. She studied Italian and French Literature at the University of Toronto. She has a Masters Degree in Education and pursuing a Masters Degree in Italian Literature. Josie won several prizes for her work in both Italian and English.

GRAHAM DUCKER is an honours graduate of Laurentian University. He spent many years as a Principal and Kindergarten Teacher in various Ontario schools. He is the author of *Don't Wake The Teacher!* and a poetry book *Observations of Heart and Mind*.

MARY CRAIG GARDNER was born in England and immigrated to Canada in her late twenties. She is a graduate of the University of Toronto. Mary's work has been published in *Reflections*, a UK poetry book, and also in the Canadian Authors Association's book of essays and short stories, *Winners*.

ZITA HINSON lives in Toronto, Ontario. She has written many poems to inspire and help women. Zita is the author of the book *Woman Reach For Your Destiny* published by her Church.

SHERRY ISAAC has found homes for several of her short stories, including publication in *Quick Brown Fox* and *New Mystery Reader*. *The Forgetting* placed first in *The Alice Munro Short Story Contest* 2009. Please visit Sherry's website www.sherryisaac.com.

MANNY JOHAL is new to the writing scene. His background is in the health sciences. This work is an excerpt from his non-fiction manuscript *Breaking Through the Bull; How God Works*. It illustrates a personal, burgeoning spiritual journey from a scientific and Sikh perspective.

NANCY JONAH has recently returned to her home in Moncton, New Brunswick after spending 4.5 years in Toronto, Ontario. She continues to be grateful for her Toronto experience which allowed her meet many wonderful people who encouraged her to continue on with her writing.

FATMATTA KANU was born and raised in Freetown, Sierra Leone, West Africa. She attended Boston University where she obtained her Master's Degree. Now retired, Fatmatta has written an

autobiography *Through the Calabash* (2008). She is also a contributing author to two anthologies: *Memoirs Around the Table* (2006) and More *Memoirs Around the Table* (2008).

PERPARIM KAPLLANI has four books published in Albania and one in Canada. He is currently working on a collection of short stories. His play *Queen Teuta of Illyria* was selected as one of 15 best plays in a worldwide competition organized by the Ministry of Culture of Albania in 2002.

DAVID KIMEL is a newcomer to Canada from Eastern Europe who strives to deliver a message of peace and love through his poems. He is the author of the poetry book *Simple Seeds* published by Author House in 2008 and is currently working on a biographic novel *Shrouded Dawns*. David also writes for several Romanian newspapers.

SHARON KNAUER is a writer and editor in Tottenham, Ontario. Her short fiction has been published in the US and two stories are upcoming in the Canadian Authors' Association anthology *Gathered Streams* (Hidden Book Press). Her novel *Red Hot Green Tomato Blues* is currently in the submission process.

BIANCA LAKOSELJAC. BA and MA, York University. Matthew Ahern Award, Literature. Taught at Ryerson University; Humber College. President: Canadian Authors Association, Toronto. Served as judge on panel, National Capital Writing Contest, 2009; Canadian Aid Literary Award Contest, 2008. Anthologies: Canadian Woman Studies, York University 2007; Expressions, White Mountain Publication 2009.

KAREN LAM is currently studying Radio and Television at Ryerson University. She is an advocate for literacy and accessibility. As a writer, editor, and producer, Karen believes our greatest asset is the power to influence change. Oranges are her motif. Visit www.amidnightmuse.com for writing, multimedia, and more!

JOHN MAAR is a Toronto writer. His eyes lit up as he spoke of his experiences when hunting crocodiles on Solomon Islands in the early sixties until someone said that he loves talking about himself. To change this perception, John is currently working on a manuscript about a person the islanders smiled with tears.

MARIA PIA MARCHELLETTA is a quadrilingual poet, writer and translator. Over 100 of her poems have been published in anthologies internationally. Maria is the second prize winner for her short story in the National Ottawa Literary Festival. Her debut poetry collections *On the Wings of Dawn* and *Banacle of Enchantment* are forthcoming.

CASSIE MCDANIEL is a poet by way of graphic design. Her forthcoming début collection of poetry *Polar Molecules* exhibits little patience for the mundane; candid pieces explore intellectual approaches to poetry as well as personal accounts from both her travels abroad and her childhood spent in the southern United States.

GEMMA MEHARCHAND was born in South Africa and now lives in Toronto where she has been persuaded by her friends at the High Park Writers' Group to come out of her writing closet and pursue her literary dreams.

BRAZ MENEZES is an architect and urban planner. He was born in Kenya and worked for 25 years with the World Bank in Washington DC, before returning to Toronto. Previously published by the World Bank, he studied at Toronto's George Brown College to learn how to write "real English" again. *The Way It Was Then* is his debut in creative non-fiction.

JATIN NAIK lives in Toronto, Ontario and works in the field of journalism and web publishing. He is a member of the Writers and Editors Network. Jatin has a passion for writing and visual arts. He has contributed his time and volunteered for many not-for-profit organizations.

LISABETH NEUMAN lives in Toronto with her husband, a criminal lawyer, their guitar playing son and cello playing daughter, two rabbits and one snake. She is currently working towards a Professional Writer's Certificate. Lisabeth loves the arts, especially the written word.

JUDY POWELL has received writing awards from Canada, USA, and Jamaica. Her writing includes essays, literary fiction and contemporary romance novels. Judy holds graduate degrees in Spanish, Marketing and Literature. She is currently pursuing the Master of Fine Arts in Creative Writing.

SYLVIA PRICE is a Toronto area writer and artist. She is currently completing her first novel and pursuing her dream of becoming a published author.

ELANA RAE is the pen name used by Debbie Rolfe. She is currently a PhD student in nursing and bioethics at the University of Toronto. Debbie's stories have been published in *Canadian Woman Studies*, *Touched by Adoption 1 &2*, and *The JCB Voice*. She lives with her family in Scarborough, Ontario.

MAHEEN A. RASHDI is an international journalist writing on South Asian issues. She has also written papers on press freedom and gender conflict for UN projects. Her co-author, **KARIM BONDREY**, an expert in oceanography, has spent his life as a master mariner, serving at sea in England and Pakistan and then continued his career as Head of Port Operations in Karachi, Pakistan.

PRATAP REDDY moved to Canada in 2002. An underwriter by day and a writer by night, he writes short fiction about the angst and the agonies (on occasion, the ecstasies) of immigrants from India. In 2008, he received the Mississauga Arts Council award for Best Emerging Literary Artist.

LARRY RODNESS lives in Toronto. He and his wife, Jodi, have been professional singers for over 30 years. Larry has written professionally for musical theatre, had 3 screenplays optioned to date, and his first fiction novel *Today I am a Man* is scheduled for release in October 2009 by Savant Books and Publications.

PHILOMENA SALDANHA was born and raised in Bombay (she refuses to call it "Mumbai"). She came to Canada in 1991. An accountant by profession, she was nudged into the writing world by her close friend, Jasmine D'Costa, and makes her debut in this anthology.

MEL SARNESE is an internationally published Toronto poet and broadcaster on the CBC and TVOntario. She is the 2009 winner of the Ted Plantos Memorial Award for her poetry, Writer in Residence at Markham Stouffville Hospital, editor of the anthology *Poetry of Relationships*. Her recent book *Leper's Cave* (Baret Days Press 2006) has been widely received.

ANDREW SCOTT is a native of Fredericton, New Brunswick. He has written three books of poetry *Here I Am*, *The Lonely Man's Road* and *The Solitary Man's Hill*. Andrew started writing as a way to communicate and cleanse his feelings. His poems are based on emotions and feelings.

MARIAN SCOTT is a Toronto writer. Her short stories have appeared in *Appleseed Quarterly*, *The Canadian Journal of Storytelling*, *Saturday High Park Writers' Anthology*, and *Seeing Red and other Stories* (published by the Writers and Editors Network). Currently Marian is working on her first collection of poetry and short stories.

REVA STERN, author of the Chapters/Indigo "Staff Choice" novel *The Water Buffalo That Shed Her Girdle*, has been published in magazines, newsletters and newspapers, and has been the recipient of several awards of merit in theatre and writing. Her next novel *"The Prescott Journals* is scheduled for publication in 2010.

SANDOR STERN published his first novel *The Life and Adventures of Ralph the Cat* in 2009 after decades as a screenwriter and director. His writing credits include *The Amityville Horror* and *Fastbreak* for which he received an NAACP Image award for best screenplay. He has also received a best dramatic episode nomination from the Writers Guild of America for *Mod Squad*.

STEVEN H. STERN received his degree from Ryerson University in Toronto and began his career at the CBC. He worked in every aspect of the Canadian entertainment industry for many years. Steven has directed over sixty motion pictures, many of which he also produced and/or wrote. His films have been shown and won awards at film festivals around the world.

ANNA STITSKI has been writing since she was old enough to hold a pencil. She writes short stories, children's stories and an occasional poem. She has also written and edited business communication materials. *Married Life* is her first published story.

HAILUN TANG is a Ph.D. and is now doing research at the University of Toronto. She published several research papers in major science magazines. Hailun is now exploring the literature world and looking to write science books for children.

LINDA TORNEY spent most of her working life in the Labour Movement, culminating in 13 years as the first woman president of the Toronto and York Region Labour Council. She took early retirement from the Labour Council to pursue a new career as a writer. In addition to *Swirling Leaves,* she has published a short story *Seeing Red* and is currently working on her second novel.

EDWIN VASAN was born in India and completed his engineering degree at the prestigious Indian Institute of Technology in Madras (now known as Chennai). He has lived in Ontario for the past 25 years in the Durham Region. Edwin is the author of his debut novel Kanishka.

HERB WARE has worked as a journalist and business writer for most of his career. He recently moved into the fiction field and is now concentrating his efforts on this genre. Herb also conducts writing workshops, critiques and editing services that help developing authors to improve their work.

KAROL ZELAZNY is an author, philosopher, and transformational speaker. *His first book Walk on Water in the World of Symptoms* was published in 2007. Karol is a certified hypnotherapist and facilitator for Silva UltraMind ESP seminars and also presents his own course. He is a program director at Radical Health Clinic.

ZOHRA ZOBERI writes drama, poetry, and fiction in English and Urdu. She is the founder of Bridging the Gap with a mission of *Enlightenment through Entertainment* which is reflected in her stage plays *Window Shopping... for lasting love* (2007 Finalist Award) and *Questionably Ever After* (Emerging Performing Arts Award for 2008 from the Mississauga Arts Council).